GAME BIRD COOKERY

CHANHASSEN, MINNESOTA

www.creativepub.com

President/CEO: Michael Eleftheriou
Vice President/Publisher: Linda Ball

GAME BIRD COOKERY

Executive Editor, Outdoor Products Group: Don Oster
Book Development Leader: Ellen C. Boeke
Managing Editor: Denise Bornhausen
Project Manager: Tracy Stanley
Editor: Janice Cauley
Advising Editor: Teresa Marrone
Associate Creative Director: Brad Springer
Art Director: Mark Jacobson
Desktop Publishing Specialist: Laurie Kristensen
Home Economists: Ellen C. Boeke, Bobbette Destiche,
  Elizabeth Emmons, Nancy Johnson
Dietitian: Hill Nutrition Associates, Inc.
V.P. Photography and Production: Jim Bindas
Studio Services Manager: Marcia Chambers
Studio Services Coordinator: Cheryl Neisen
Lead Photographer: Rex Irmen
Contributing Photographers: Billy Lindner, Chuck Nields, Steve Smith,
  Greg Wallace
Lead Food Stylist: Bobbette Destiche
Food Stylists: Elizabeth Emmons, Nancy Johnson, Karen Linden
Contributors: Tom Carpenter, Teresa Marrone, Don Oster, David Payne,
  Susan Spicer
Production Manager: Kim Gerber
Production Staff: Curt Ellering, Laura Hokkanen, Kay Wethern

Printing: R. R. Donnelley
10 9 8 7 6 5 4 3 2

Copyright © 1997 by Creative Publishing international, Inc.
18705 Lake Drive East
Chanhassen, MN 55317
1-800-328-3895
www.creativepub.com

Library of Congress Cataloging-in-Publication Data
Game bird cookery.
    p. cm. -- (The hunting and fishing library)
    ISBN 0-86573-070-9 (hardcover)
    1. Cookery (Poultry) 2. Cookery (Game)
I. Cowles Creative Publishing. II. Title: The complete hunter
III. Series.
TX750.G35 1997
641.6'65--dc21   97-24704

Contents

Introduction 4

Upland Birds 9
    Turkey 11
    Pheasant 14
    Light-Medium Birds 31
    Dark-Medium Birds 44
    Light-Small Birds 58
    Dark-Small Birds 71

Waterfowl 79
    Goose 80
    Puddle Ducks 95
    Diving Ducks 108
    Tiny Ducks 120

Index 124

Introduction

Game Bird Cookery is an all-new collection of over 150 recipes for all types of North American game birds. Each recipe has been carefully tested and written with detailed instructions to ensure success when you are preparing your own game birds. This book contains everything from classic roasted wild turkey to unique and contemporary recipes sure to suit everyone's taste.

In addition to great bird recipes, each section features a special menu with side-dish recipes and serving suggestions. These menus let you showcase your prized game birds for family and friends.

Game Bird Cookery is divided into ten sections based on the type of bird (upland game bird or waterfowl), its size and the color of its meat. We have come up with working terms in the upland game bird category that combine birds of similar size and meat color. These are described below.

Turkey and Pheasant are independent sections. Turkey is the largest of the game birds, and cannot be easily classed with any other bird. And pheasant's popularity demands that it be given special consideration in a section of its own.

The Light-Medium Birds section describes medium-size upland game birds with light-colored meat. These birds are generally less strong in flavor and somewhat drier than dark-meated birds. Birds included in this category are chukar partridge, ruffed grouse and blue grouse. Light-Small Birds includes birds with light meat that are small in size. All types of quail are included in this category.

Dark-Medium Birds includes Hungarian partridge, prairie chicken, sharptail grouse, sage grouse and spruce grouse. They are similar in size to the light-medium birds, but their meat is darker and stronger tasting. Dark-Small Birds includes birds that are small in size with dark, flavorful meat. All doves and woodcock are included in this category.

Waterfowl make up the remaining four categories. The first is Goose, which includes the Canada goose, snow or blue goose and the white-fronted goose.

Ducks were separated into three categories, based on their size and feeding habits. Puddle Ducks includes mallard, black duck, pintail, gadwall, wigeon and wood duck. Diving Ducks includes canvasback, redhead, greater scaup, lesser scaup, ring-necked, goldeneye and bufflehead. Diving ducks are bottom feeders, so they have a strong flavor. Tiny Ducks includes all teals, which are in a category of their own since they are so much smaller than other ducks.

Nutritional Analysis

Each recipe includes nutrition information and exchanges for weight management. If a recipe has a range of servings, the data applies to the greater number of servings. If alternate ingredients are listed, the analysis applies to the first ingredient listed; optional ingredients are not included in the analysis.

All recipes for turkey, goose, pheasant and quail were done with the bird specified, though wild bird data is not always available. Since nutritional data on some species is not available, appropriate substitutions were made in order to give you a close estimate of nutritional information.

Goose and turkey analyses were done with data for domestic geese and turkey, which are not as lean as their wild counterparts. Squab data was used for dove recipes. Analyses for ducks were done with wild duck data, and the same data was used for all ducks. All other game birds were analyzed using pheasant data. Data for raw meat was used when cooked meat data was not available.

Icons

The following icons can be found throughout this book to help you in meal planning.

FAST FAST (45 to 30 minutes or less for preparation and cooking)

VERY FAST VERY FAST (30 minutes or less for preparation and cooking)

LOW-FAT LOW-FAT (10 or fewer grams of fat per serving)

Substitution Chart

Although game birds differ in size, flavor and texture, they can be substituted one for another in a recipe. But when substituting, keep these differences in mind and expect the end results to vary. For example, substituting a light-meated bird like chukar partridge for pheasant will not alter a recipe a great deal. But if you use sharptail grouse for ruffed grouse, be prepared for a vastly different result, since sharptail meat is very dark and strong-flavored compared to the dry, delicate light meat of a ruffed grouse.

Keep in mind, too, that cooking times will vary depending on the size of the substitute bird and its age. If a recipe calls for a whole bird, it is best to substitute a bird of similar size in order to ensure that cooking times will be accurate. Pieces of similar size can be freely substituted. Older birds and some birds in a different category will be tougher and dryer than those called for in recipes. When substituting older, drier birds, choose a recipe that requires long cooking with a moist-cooking technique.

We have taken a "mix-and-match" approach to substitution in our chart (opposite). It will help you match specific birds of similar size and/or meat type. The chart is broken into eight areas. If you don't have the particular type of bird called for in a recipe, just locate that bird on the chart and substitute any other bird of similar size from that same area of the chart.

AREA	SPECIES	APPROXIMATE DRESSED WEIGHT	NUMBER OF SERVINGS
Large Upland Birds	*Wild Turkey*		
	whole	8 to 16 lbs.	5 to 10
	pieces	3 to 4½ lbs.	6 to 8
Light-Medium Upland Birds	Pheasant	1½ to 2¼ lbs.	3 to 4
	Blue Grouse	1 to 2¼ lbs.	2 to 4
	Ruffed Grouse	¾ to 1 lb.	2
	Chukar Partridge	¾ to 1 lb.	2
Dark-Medium Upland Birds	Sage Grouse	2¼ to 4 lbs.	4 to 7
	Prairie Chicken	1 to 2¼ lbs.	2 to 4
	Sharptail Grouse	1 to 1¼ lbs.	2 to 3
	Hungarian Partridge	¾ to 1 lb.	2
	Spruce Grouse	¾ to 1 lb.	2
Light-Small Upland Birds	Quail	4 to 6 oz.	1
Dark-Small Upland Birds	Woodcock	5 oz. each	1
	Dove	2 doves (2 to 3 oz. each)	1
Geese	*Giant Canada*		
	Young	4 to 6 lbs.	4 to 6
	Mature	6½ to 10 lbs.	6 to 10
	Interior Canada		
	Young	3½ to 4½ lbs.	4 to 5
	Mature	4¾ to 6 lbs.	5 to 10
	Lesser Canada	3 to 4½ lbs.	3 to 6
	Snow or Blue Goose	3 to 4 lbs.	3 to 5
	White-fronted Goose	3½ to 3¾ lbs.	3 to 5
Large Ducks	Canvasback	1¾ lbs.	2
	Mallard	1¼ to 1½ lbs.	2
	Black Duck	1¼ to 1½ lbs.	2
	Redhead	1¼ lbs.	2
	Greater Scaup (Bluebill)	1¼ lbs.	2
Small Ducks	Goldeneye	1 to 1¼ lbs.	1 to 1½
	Pintail	1 to 1¼ lbs.	1 to 1½
	Gadwall	¾ to 1 lb.	1 to 1½
	Wigeon	¾ to 1 lb.	1 to 1½
	Lesser Scaup	¾ to 1 lb.	1 to 1½
	Ring-necked	¾ lb.	1 to 1½
	Wood Duck	½ to ¾ lb.	1
	Bufflehead	5 oz. to ¾ lb.	1
	Blue-winged Teal	½ lb.	1
	Cinnamon Teal	5 oz. to ½ lb.	1
	Green-winged Teal	5 to 6 oz.	1 or less

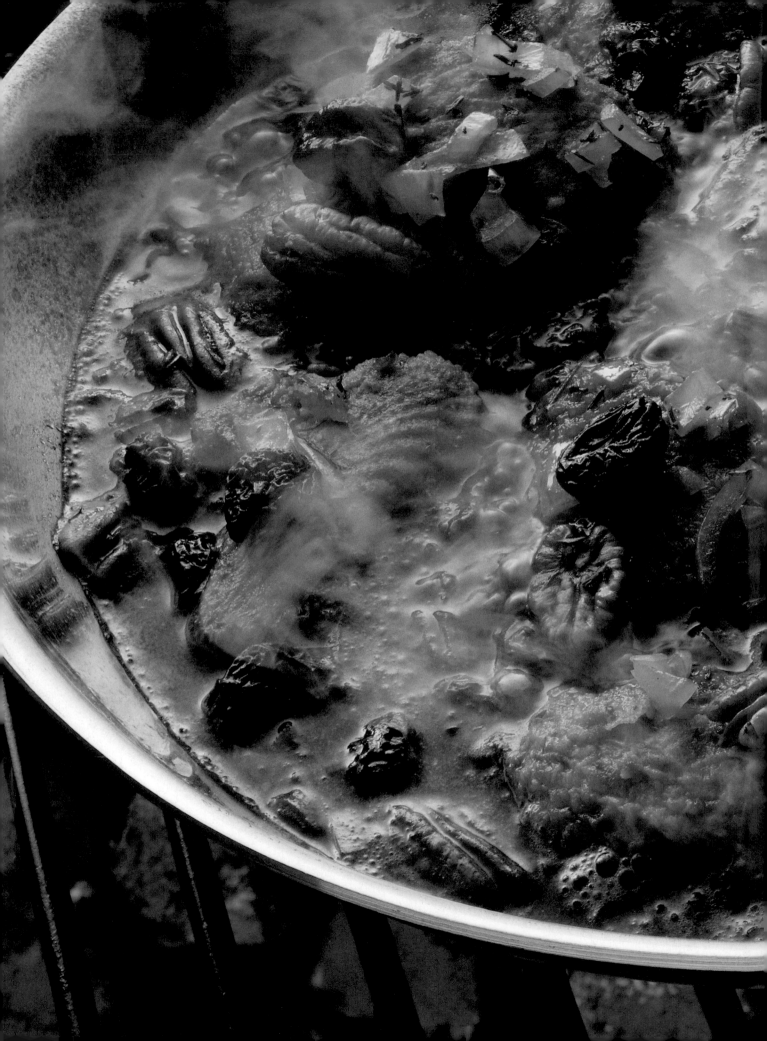

Turkey

Menu

Roasted Wild Turkey (recipe below)

Cranberry Corn Bread Dressing (recipe below) ❧ *Pumpkin Soup (recipe below)*

Wild Rice Blend with Toasted Almonds ❧ *Corn*

Roasted Wild Turkey

An oven bag is an excellent tool when roasting wild birds, such as turkey. It helps keep an otherwise lean and dry bird moist.

1 tablespoon all-purpose flour
1 whole dressed wild turkey
    (8 to 10 lbs.), skin on
    Salt and pepper to taste
2 stalks celery, cut into 3-inch
    pieces
1 medium onion, quartered
3 tablespoons vegetable oil

6 to 8 servings

Heat oven to 350°F. Add 1 table-spoon flour to turkey-size (23½ × 19-inch) oven cooking bag; shake to distribute. Place cooking bag in 13 × 9-inch roasting pan.

Season cavity of turkey with salt and pepper. Place celery and onion in cavity of turkey. Tuck tips of wings behind turkey's back. Truss legs with kitchen string. Brush entire turkey with oil. Place turkey in cooking bag; secure bag with provided nylon tie. Insert meat thermometer into thickest part of thigh through top of bag. Make six ½-inch slits in top of bag.

Roast turkey for 2 to 2½ hours, or until internal temperature reads 180°F. Remove turkey from bag. Let stand, tented with foil, for 20 minutes before carving.

Per Serving: Calories: 608 • Protein: 82 g.
• Carbohydrate: 1 g. • Fat: 28 g.
• Cholesterol: 239 mg. • Sodium: 212 mg.
Exchanges: 11 lean meat

Pumpkin Soup 🔹LOW-FAT

4 cups ready-to-serve chicken
    broth, divided
1 medium carrot, chopped
    (½ cup)
1 stalk celery, sliced (½ cup)
¼ cup chopped onion
1 can (16 oz.) pumpkin
½ cup dry white wine
½ teaspoon dried thyme leaves
⅛ teaspoon pepper

6 to 8 servings

In 3-quart saucepan, combine 1 cup broth, the carrot, celery and onion. Bring to a boil over medium-high heat. Cover. Reduce heat to low. Simmer for 12 to 15 minutes, or until vegetables are tender. Remove from heat. Cool slightly.

In food processor or blender, process vegetable mixture until smooth. Return mixture to saucepan. Stir in remaining ingredients. Cook over medium heat for 10 to 15 minutes, or until mixture is heated through and begins to simmer, stirring occasionally.

Per Serving: Calories: 58 • Protein: 2 g. • Carbohydrate: 7 g. • Fat: 1 g.
• Cholesterol: 0 mg. • Sodium: 586 mg.
Exchanges: ¼ starch, 1 vegetable, ¼ fat

Cranberry Corn Bread Dressing

2 tablespoons butter or margarine
¾ cup chopped onion
¾ cup sliced celery
6 cups dried corn bread
    stuffing mix
1½ cups water or chicken broth
1 cup dried cranberries
½ cup chopped walnuts
1¼ teaspoons poultry seasoning
½ teaspoon salt
¼ teaspoon freshly ground
    pepper

6 to 8 servings

Heat oven to 350°F. Spray 3-quart casserole with nonstick vegetable cooking spray. Set aside. In 1-quart saucepan, melt butter over medium heat. Add onion and celery. Cook for 3 to 5 minutes, or until vegetables are tender-crisp, stirring occasionally. Remove from heat.

In large mixing bowl, combine onion mixture, stuffing mix, water, cranberries and walnuts. Toss lightly to coat. Add poultry seasoning, salt and pepper. Toss to combine. Spoon mixture into prepared casserole. Cover. Bake for 30 minutes. Uncover. Bake for 10 to 15 minutes longer, or until top is golden brown.

TIP: Bake dressing with the turkey.

Per Serving: Calories: 383 • Protein: 8 g. • Carbohydrate: 65 g. • Fat: 10 g.
• Cholesterol: 8 mg. • Sodium: 922 mg.
Exchanges: 3½ starch, ¾ fruit, 2 fat

Barbecue-smoked Turkey

RUB MIX:

- ½ cup catsup
- 2 tablespoons packed brown sugar
- 1 tablespoon prepared yellow mustard
- 1 tablespoon Worcestershire sauce
- 1 teaspoon chili powder
- 1 teaspoon salt
- 1 teaspoon hot pepper sauce
- ½ teaspoon garlic powder
- ½ teaspoon freshly ground pepper
- 1 whole dressed wild turkey (8 to 10 lbs.), skin on
  Hickory wood chips
  Hot water, chicken broth or beer

6 to 8 servings

In small mixing bowl, combine rub mix ingredients. Spread mixture evenly in cavity and over surface of turkey. Let turkey air dry for 45 minutes. Soak wood chips in warm water for 30 minutes; drain. Heat smoker to 200°F.

Position smoker rack at lowest setting in smoker. Fill 13 × 9-inch pan half full with hot liquid and place on rack. Spray second smoker rack with nonstick vegetable cooking spray. Place prepared rack at position just above water pan. Place turkey breast-side-up on rack above pan. Place chips in smoker.

Smoke turkey for 6 to 8 hours, or until internal temperature in thickest part of breast registers 180°F. Keep smoker temperature between 200° and 250°F, and refill water pan, if necessary.

Per Serving: Calories: 491 • Protein: 64 g.
• Carbohydrate: 8 g. • Fat: 21 g.
• Cholesterol: 186 mg. • Sodium: 682 mg.
Exchanges: 9 very lean meat, 4 fat

Pecan Turkey with Maple Sauce ↑

- ¼ cup pure maple syrup
- 2 tablespoons dark corn syrup
- 3 tablespoons applejack brandy
- 1 tablespoon butter, melted
- 1 whole bone-in wild turkey breast (3 to 4 lbs.), skin on
- ¾ cup finely chopped pecans

6 to 8 servings

Heat oven to 350°F. In small bowl, combine syrups, brandy and butter. Reserve ¼ cup mixture. Set remaining mixture aside. Place turkey breast skin-side-up in roasting pan. Brush evenly with 2 tablespoons reserved syrup mixture. Press pecans evenly over breast to coat. Cover with foil.

Bake for 1 hour 15 minutes. Brush remaining 2 tablespoons reserved mixture over breast. Bake, uncovered, for 15 to 30 minutes, or until internal temperature registers 180°F in thickest part of breast. Serve with remaining syrup mixture.

Per Serving: Calories: 389 • Protein: 40 g. • Carbohydrate: 14 g. • Fat: 18 g.
• Cholesterol: 105 mg. • Sodium: 109 mg.
Exchanges: 5½ very lean meat, 3½ fat

Turkey Stew with Dumplings

- 3 tablespoons butter or margarine
- 4 medium carrots, sliced (2 cups)
- ¼ cup chopped onion
- ¼ cup all-purpose flour
- 2 cups ready-to-serve chicken broth
- 1⅔ cups 2% milk, divided
- 3 cups (12 oz.) chopped cooked wild turkey
- 1 cup frozen peas, defrosted
- ½ cup frozen corn kernels, defrosted
- ½ teaspoon dried thyme leaves
- ½ teaspoon salt
- ½ teaspoon pepper
- 2 cups buttermilk baking mix
- ½ teaspoon snipped fresh rosemary leaves (or ¼ teaspoon crushed dried rosemary)

4 to 6 servings

Heat oven to 400°F. Spray 11 × 7-inch baking dish with nonstick vegetable cooking spray. Set aside. In 3-quart saucepan, melt butter over medium heat. Add carrots and onion. Cook for 3 to 5 minutes, or until vegetables are tender-crisp, stirring occasionally. Stir in flour. Cook for 1 minute, stirring constantly. Gradually blend in broth and 1 cup milk. Cook for 5 to 6 minutes, or until mixture is thickened and bubbly, stirring constantly.

Remove from heat. Stir in turkey, peas, corn, thyme, salt and pepper. Spoon mixture into prepared dish. Set aside. In small mixing bowl, combine baking mix, remaining ⅔ cup milk and the rosemary; stir just until moistened. Drop batter onto turkey mixture by spoonfuls to form 6 dumplings. Bake for 30 to 35 minutes, or until stew is hot and bubbly and dumplings are golden brown.

Per Serving: Calories: 430 • Protein: 25 g. • Carbohydrate: 43 g. • Fat: 17 g. • Cholesterol: 65 mg. • Sodium: 1181 mg. Exchanges: 2¼ starch, 2 very lean meat, 1 vegetable, ¼ low-fat milk, 3 fat

Turkey Chowder LOW-FAT ↑

- 1 cup water
- 1 large potato, peeled and cut into ¼-inch cubes (1 cup)
- 1 medium onion, chopped (1 cup)
- 2 teaspoons chicken bouillon granules
- 1 clove garlic, minced
- ¼ teaspoon pepper
- 2 cups 2% milk
- 1 can (15 oz.) cream-style corn
- 1 can (4 oz.) diced green chilies
- ¾ to 1 teaspoon ground cumin
- 1½ cups (6 oz.) chopped cooked wild turkey
- 1 medium tomato, seeded and chopped (1 cup)
- ¾ cup (3 oz.) shredded Colby-Jack cheese or Cheddar cheese

6 servings

In 3-quart saucepan, combine water, potato, onion, bouillon, garlic and pepper. Bring to a boil over medium-high heat, stirring occasionally. Reduce heat to medium-low. Simmer for 12 to 15 minutes, or until vegetables are tender.

Stir in milk, corn, chilies and cumin. Increase heat to medium. Cook for 10 to 15 minutes, or until mixture is very hot, stirring occasionally. Stir in turkey. Cook for 4 to 6 minutes, or until turkey is heated through, stirring occasionally. To serve, top each serving evenly with tomato and cheese.

Per Serving: Calories: 241 • Protein: 17 g. • Carbohydrate: 27 g. • Fat: 8 g. • Cholesterol: 41 mg. • Sodium: 827 mg. Exchanges: 1¼ starch, 1½ very lean meat, 1 vegetable, ¼ low-fat milk, 1¼ fat

Pheasant

Menu

Chicken-fried Pheasant (recipe below)

Garlic Mashed Potatoes (recipe below) ❧ *Buttermilk Biscuits*

Steamed Snow Pea Pods

Chicken-fried Pheasant

This is a traditional, southern-style treatment of pheasant.

1/3 cup 2% milk
1 egg
1/3 cup all-purpose flour
1/2 teaspoon salt
1/4 teaspoon pepper
1 dressed pheasant (1 1/2 to
   2 1/4 lbs.), cut up, skin on

2 tablespoons butter
2 tablespoons vegetable oil

GRAVY:
1 1/4 cups 2% milk
2 tablespoons all-purpose flour
1/4 teaspoon salt
   Dash pepper

3 to 4 servings

In shallow dish, combine 1/3 cup milk and the egg. In large sealable plastic bag, combine 1/3 cup flour, 1/2 teaspoon salt and 1/4 teaspoon pepper. Dip pheasant pieces in milk mixture, then place in bag, shaking to coat. Set aside.

In 12-inch skillet, heat butter and oil over medium-high heat. Add pheasant pieces. Cook for 10 to 12 minutes, or until meat is tender and juices run clear, turning pieces occasionally. (If pheasant starts to overbrown, reduce heat to medium.) Set pieces aside on heated platter and keep warm.

In small bowl, combine gravy ingredients. Whisk mixture into skillet drippings. Cook over medium-low heat for 1 to 2 minutes, or until gravy is thickened and bubbly. Serve gravy with pheasant.

Per Serving: Calories: 563 • Protein: 48 g. • Carbohydrate: 16 g. • Fat: 33 g.
• Cholesterol: 207 mg. • Sodium: 605 mg.
Exchanges: 3/4 starch, 6 lean meat, 1/2 low-fat milk, 2 1/2 fat

Garlic Mashed Potatoes

4 medium russet potatoes, peeled
   and cut into 1-inch cubes
   (3 cups)
5 whole cloves garlic, peeled
   Water
1/3 cup warm 2% milk
2 tablespoons butter or margarine
   Salt and pepper to taste

3 to 4 servings

In 2-quart saucepan, combine potatoes and garlic. Add water to just cover potatoes. Bring to a boil over high heat. Reduce heat to medium. Simmer for 10 to 12 minutes, or until potatoes are tender. Drain.

Add milk, butter, salt and pepper to pan. Mash mixture with potato masher or electric mixer until desired texture. Transfer to warm serving bowl.

Per Serving: Calories: 157 • Protein: 3 g.
• Carbohydrate: 22 g. • Fat: 6 g.
• Cholesterol: 17 mg. • Sodium: 78 mg.
Exchanges: 1 1/2 starch, 1 1/4 fat

Herb-coated Roast Pheasant

3 cups loosely packed fresh mixed
   herbs (curly-leaf parsley, flat-
   leaf parsley, sorrel, tarragon,
   dill weed)
1 whole dressed pheasant (1½ to
   2¼ lbs.), skin on, trussed*

1 egg yolk, beaten
   Salt and pepper to taste
2 tablespoons butter, softened
1 cup water, divided

3 to 4 servings

Heat oven to 375°F. In food processor or with chef's knife, finely chop
herbs. Set aside. Place pheasant breast-side-up in small roasting pan.
Brush with yolk. Sprinkle evenly with salt and pepper. Pat herb mixture
evenly over pheasant. Dot pheasant evenly with butter. Pour ½ cup water
in bottom of roasting pan.

Roast pheasant for 50 minutes to 1 hour, or until pheasant is tender and
juices run clear, basting occasionally with pan juices. Remove pheasant
from oven, draining any juices in cavity of bird into pan. Place pheasant
on serving platter and keep warm.

Place roasting pan over medium-high heat. Add remaining ½ cup water
to pan, scraping bottom of pan to remove any browned bits. Bring to a
boil. Boil for 4 to 5 minutes, or until liquid is reduced to desired thickness. Strain liquid. Pour over pheasant.

Per Serving: Calories: 421 • Protein: 44 g. • Carbohydrate: 5 g. • Fat: 24 g.
• Cholesterol: 199 mg. • Sodium: 160 mg.
Exchanges: 6 lean meat, 1 vegetable, 1¼ fat

How to Truss a Pheasant

METHOD 1: Secure the legs together,
using kitchen string.

METHOD 2: Cut a hole in the skin of
the pheasant at the base of the tail, and
tuck the ends of legs into the hole.

Cranberry-glazed Pheasant

1 whole dressed pheasant (1½ to 2¼ lbs.), skin on, trussed*
2 tablespoons butter, melted
  Salt and pepper to taste
1 lb. fresh or frozen cranberries
1 cup sugar
1 cup orange juice
¼ cup orange-flavored liqueur
2 tablespoons grated orange peel
  Orange slices and cranberries
    for garnish

3 to 4 servings

Per Serving: Calories: 688 • Protein: 43 g.
• Carbohydrate: 76 g. • Fat: 23 g.
• Cholesterol: 146 mg. • Sodium: 134 mg.
Exchanges: 6 lean meat, 1½ fruit, 1 fat

Heat oven to 350°F. Place pheasant breast-side-up in small roasting pan. Brush with melted butter. Sprinkle evenly with salt and pepper. Cover pan with foil. Roast for 45 minutes.

Meanwhile, in 2-quart saucepan, combine cranberries, sugar and juice. Bring to a boil over high heat. Reduce heat to low. Simmer for 10 minutes, stirring frequently. Stir in liqueur and peel. Simmer for 5 minutes longer, stirring frequently. Remove glaze from heat.

Remove foil from pheasant. Spoon 1 cup glaze over pheasant. Continue roasting, uncovered, for 20 to 25 minutes, or until pheasant is tender and golden brown and juices run clear, basting frequently with pan juices.

Remove pheasant from oven and place on warm serving platter. Spoon ½ cup of remaining glaze over pheasant. Garnish with orange slices and cranberries. Serve remaining glaze with pheasant.

See trussing technique (opposite).

Grill-smoked Pheasant

BRINE:

6 cups cold water

½ cup plus 1 tablespoon canning/pickling salt

¼ cup plus 2 tablespoons packed brown sugar

3 tablespoons maple syrup

2 tablespoons plus 1 teaspoon white wine vinegar

2 teaspoons pickling spice

1 whole dressed pheasant (1½ to 2¼ lbs.), skin on
Apple or cherry wood chips

2 tablespoons honey

2 teaspoons soy sauce
Hot chicken broth, beer or water

3 to 4 servings

Per Serving: Calories: 379 • Protein: 42 g. • Carbohydrate: 12 g. • Fat: 17 g. • Cholesterol: 131 mg. • Sodium: 1041 mg. Exchanges: 6 lean meat

In large nonmetallic bowl or sealable plastic bag, combine brine ingredients. Stir until salt and sugar are dissolved. Add pheasant. Cover. Chill 4 hours, turning pheasant once or twice. Drain and discard brine from pheasant. Pat pheasant dry with paper towels. Let pheasant air dry for 30 minutes.

While pheasant is air drying, start large load of charcoal briquettes on one side of charcoal grill. Soak wood chips in warm water for 30 minutes; drain. In small bowl, combine honey and soy sauce. When briquettes are covered with light ash, toss a handful of wood chips on them. Place pan ⅔ full of hot broth on cooking grid over charcoal. Brush pheasant with honey mixture and place it on opposite side of cooking grid. Cover grill.

Smoke pheasant for 2 to 3 hours, or until pheasant is fully cooked. (Do not open grill unless necessary.) Temperature in grill should stay between 150° and 200°F. Regulate temperature using vents on grill. Add more wood chips during the last hour of smoking.

TIP: To monitor temperature in grill, clip a deep-frying thermometer into a clothespin and insert the tip into a vent hole in the lid of the grill. The clothespin keeps the thermometer from coming in contact with hot metal.

Creamed Pheasant & Biscuits *LOW-FAT*

This classic recipe is a perennial favorite and a real comfort food. Serve it on a cold, blustery day.

    7 cups water
    1 whole dressed pheasant (1½ to
       2¼ lbs.), skin removed
    1 medium carrot, cut into 1-inch
       lengths
    1 stalk celery, cut into 1-inch
       lengths
    1 small onion, cut into 8 wedges
    1 bay leaf
    6 peppercorns
   ½ cup all-purpose flour
    1 cup 2% milk
       Salt and pepper to taste
    6 buttermilk biscuits

                              6 servings

In 4-quart saucepan, combine water, pheasant, carrot, celery, onion, bay leaf and peppercorns. Bring to a boil over high heat. Cover. Reduce heat to medium-low. Simmer for 45 minutes to 1 hour, or until pheasant is tender.

Remove pheasant from pot; set aside to cool slightly. Strain stock through fine-mesh sieve. Discard vegetables and bay leaf. Set 2 cups of stock aside. Reserve remaining stock for future use. Remove pheasant meat from bones; discard bones. Coarsely shred meat. Set aside.

Return reserved 2 cups stock to saucepan. Bring to a simmer over medium heat. Place flour in small mixing bowl. Blend milk into flour. Whisk milk mixture into stock in saucepan. Stir in pheasant. Cook for 3 to 4 minutes, or until mixture is thickened and bubbly, stirring constantly. Add salt and pepper to taste. Serve creamed pheasant over split biscuits.

Per Serving: Calories: 303 • Protein: 24 g. • Carbohydrate: 29 g. • Fat: 10 g. • Cholesterol: 57 mg. • Sodium: 424 mg. Exchanges: 1¾ starch, 2¾ very lean meat, 2 fat

Fruity Garlic-roasted Pheasant ↑

   ½ cup brandy or cognac, divided
   ⅓ cup raisins
   ⅓ cup dried cranberries
    1 whole dressed pheasant (1½
       to 2¼ lbs.), skin on
    1 clove garlic, crushed

       Salt and pepper to taste
    2 sprigs fresh sage
    8 whole cloves garlic, peeled
   1¼ cups dry red wine, divided
    1 teaspoon honey

                            3 to 4 servings

In small bowl, combine ⅓ cup brandy, the raisins and cranberries. Let soak for several hours or overnight.

Heat oven to 375°F. Rinse pheasant and pat dry with paper towels. Rub surface of pheasant with crushed garlic. Sprinkle surface and cavity with salt and pepper. Place sage sprigs in pheasant cavity, and truss pheasant (see trussing technique on page 16). Place pheasant in small roasting pan. Arrange whole garlic cloves around pheasant. Pour 1 cup wine and raisin mixture into pan around pheasant.

Roast pheasant for 50 minutes to 1 hour, or until meat is tender and juices run clear, basting occasionally with pan juices. Remove pheasant from oven, draining any juices in cavity of bird into pan. Place pheasant on serving platter and keep warm.

Place roasting pan over medium-high heat. Add remaining ¼ cup wine and remaining brandy to pan, scraping bottom of pan to remove any browned bits. Bring to a boil. Boil for 5 to 6 minutes, or until liquid is reduced to desired thickness. Whisk in honey. Spoon sauce around pheasant on platter.

TIP: To speed-soak raisins and cranberries, cover the bowl containing the brandy and fruit with plastic wrap. Microwave at High for 1 minute. Let stand for 30 minutes.

Per Serving: Calories: 455 • Protein: 43 g. • Carbohydrate: 22 g. • Fat: 17 g. • Cholesterol: 131 mg. • Sodium: 80 mg. Exchanges: 6 lean meat, 1 fruit

Mediterranean Pheasant with Onions

2 dressed pheasants (1½ to 2¼ lbs. each), quartered, skin removed
1 tablespoon rubbed sage
¼ teaspoon freshly ground pepper
¼ teaspoon salt
⅛ teaspoon ground nutmeg
⅛ teaspoon ground cinnamon
¼ cup fresh lemon juice
1 large red onion, thinly sliced
½ cup ready-to-serve chicken broth, divided
2 tablespoons extra-virgin olive oil, divided
3 pita loaves (6-inch), torn
¼ cup pine nuts, toasted*

6 to 8 servings

Per Serving: Calories: 348 • Protein: 42 g.
• Carbohydrate: 17 g. • Fat: 12 g.
• Cholesterol: 107 mg. • Sodium: 314 mg.
Exchanges: 1 starch, 5½ very lean meat,
¼ vegetable, 2½ fat

Rinse pheasant pieces and pat dry with paper towels. In small bowl, combine sage, pepper, salt, nutmeg and cinnamon. Rub 2 teaspoons of mixture evenly on pheasant. Cover pheasant with plastic wrap and chill at least 4 hours or overnight. Add remaining spice mixture to juice. Set aside.

Heat oven to 400°F. In 12-inch skillet, combine juice mixture, onion, ¼ cup broth and 1½ tablespoons oil. Bring to a boil over medium-high heat. Cover. Reduce heat to low. Simmer for 15 to 20 minutes, or until onion is very tender, stirring occasionally. Remove from heat.

Spray large baking sheet with nonstick vegetable cooking spray. Arrange pheasant pieces on prepared baking sheet. Arrange onion mixture evenly over pheasant. Cover with foil. Bake for 25 minutes.

Brush 13 × 9-inch baking dish with remaining 1½ teaspoons oil. Spread torn pitas evenly in bottom of dish. Sprinkle with remaining ¼ cup broth. Top with onion from skillet. Arrange pheasant pieces over onion. Pour juices from skillet over pheasant. Bake, uncovered, for 20 to 25 minutes, or until pheasant is browned and juices run clear. Sprinkle with pine nuts before serving.

To toast pine nuts, place them in a dry skillet over medium-low heat, until lightly browned, shaking pan occasionally.

Pheasant with Dried Cherries & Pecans ● FAST →

- ½ cup all-purpose flour
- ¼ teaspoon garlic powder
- ¼ teaspoon salt
- ¼ teaspoon pepper
- 1 dressed pheasant (1½ to 2¼ lbs.), cut up, skin removed
- 3 tablespoons vegetable oil
- 1⅔ cups dry sherry
- 1 small onion, chopped (½ cup)
- ½ cup ready-to-serve chicken broth
- 1½ teaspoons dried thyme leaves
- ½ cup dried cherries
- ½ cup pecan halves

3 to 4 servings

In shallow dish, combine flour, garlic powder, salt and pepper. Dredge pheasant pieces in flour mixture to coat. In 12-inch skillet, heat oil over medium-high heat. Add pheasant and cook for 4 to 6 minutes, or until browned, turning pieces occasionally. Remove pheasant from skillet. Wipe out skillet.

In same skillet, combine sherry, onion, broth and thyme. Add pheasant pieces. Bring to a boil over high heat. Cover. Reduce heat to medium-low. Simmer for 10 to 12 minutes, or until pheasant is tender and juices run clear. Add cherries and pecans to skillet. Cover. Simmer for 10 minutes longer.

Per Serving: Calories: 526 • Protein: 42 g. • Carbohydrate: 33 g. • Fat: 26 g. • Cholesterol: 107 mg. • Sodium: 331 mg. Exchanges: 1 starch, 5 very lean meat, ¾ fruit, 5 fat

Sherry-Cream Pheasant

- ⅔ cup all-purpose flour
- ½ teaspoon salt
- ½ teaspoon pepper
- ¼ teaspoon ground thyme
- 1 dressed pheasant (1½ to 2¼ lbs.), quartered, skin removed
- ½ cup vegetable oil
- 1 cup ready-to-serve chicken broth
- ¼ cup finely chopped onion
- 1 cup heavy whipping cream
- 1 cup sliced fresh mushrooms
- ½ cup dry sherry
- 4 cups hot cooked white and wild rice blend

4 servings

Heat oven to 350°F. In shallow dish, combine flour, salt, pepper and thyme. Dredge pheasant pieces in flour mixture to coat. In 12-inch skillet, heat oil over medium-high heat. Add pheasant. Cook for 5 to 6 minutes, or until browned, turning pieces over once. Drain pheasant on paper-towel-lined plates.

Arrange pheasant pieces in 10-inch square baking dish. Add broth and onion. Cover and bake for 1 hour. Add cream, mushrooms and sherry to dish. Bake, uncovered, for 1½ hours, or until pheasant is tender and liquid is slightly reduced. Serve over rice.

Per Serving: Calories: 866 • Protein: 49 g. • Carbohydrate: 63 g. • Fat: 47 g. • Cholesterol: 199 mg. • Sodium: 1287 mg. Exchanges: 4 starch, 5 very lean meat, ¼ vegetable, 8½ fat

Cajun Pheasant Fingers

SPICE MIX:

2½ teaspoons garlic powder
2 teaspoons dried thyme leaves
1½ teaspoons black pepper
1 to 2 teaspoons cayenne
1 teaspoon white pepper
½ teaspoon salt

1 cup apricot preserves
¼ cup Dijon mustard
2 whole boneless skinless
  pheasant breasts (5 to 6 oz.
  each), cut lengthwise into
  1-inch-wide strips
2 tablespoons vegetable oil
1 tablespoon butter or
  margarine

3 to 4 servings

In shallow dish, combine spice mix ingredients. Set aside. In 1-quart saucepan, combine preserves and mustard. Cook over medium heat for 4 to 5 minutes, or until mixture bubbles and becomes smooth, stirring frequently. Set sauce aside and keep warm.

Dredge pheasant strips in spice mix to coat. In 12-inch skillet, heat oil and butter over medium heat. Add pheasant strips. Cook for 4 to 5 minutes, or until browned, turning strips over once. Remove strips from skillet and drain on paper-towel-lined plate. Serve strips with apricot sauce for dipping.

Per Serving: Calories: 412 • Protein: 20 g.
• Carbohydrate: 55 g. • Fat: 13 g.
• Cholesterol: 53 mg. • Sodium: 722 mg.
Exchanges: 2¾ very lean meat, 2½ fat

Dijon Pheasant Legs

¼ cup Dijon mustard
2 tablespoons dry sherry
¾ cup seasoned bread crumbs
¼ cup shredded fresh Parmesan
  cheese
2 tablespoons snipped fresh
  parsley
1 teaspoon dried basil leaves

½ teaspoon dried oregano leaves
½ teaspoon garlic powder
4 bone-in pheasant leg-thigh
  quarters (4 oz. each), skin
  removed
2 tablespoons margarine or
  butter, melted

4 servings

Heat oven to 350°F. Spray 10-inch square baking dish with nonstick vegetable cooking spray. Set aside. In shallow dish, combine mustard and sherry. In second shallow dish, combine bread crumbs, Parmesan cheese, parsley, basil, oregano and garlic powder. Dip pheasant pieces in mustard mixture, then dredge in crumb mixture to coat.

Arrange pheasant pieces in prepared baking dish. Drizzle evenly with melted margarine. Bake, uncovered, for 45 to 50 minutes, or until meat is tender and juices run clear.

Per Serving: Calories: 269 • Protein: 21 g. • Carbohydrate: 17 g. • Fat: 11 g.
• Cholesterol: 47 mg. • Sodium: 1162 mg.
Exchanges: 1 starch, 2½ lean meat, ½ fat

Pheasant Saltimbocca VERY FAST

Saltimbocca (Italian for "jump in the mouth") is an Italian specialty made of veal scallops sprinkled with sage and topped with prosciutto ham, then braised in white wine. We've prepared it with pheasant breasts.

2 whole boneless skinless
   pheasant breasts (5 to 6 oz.
   each), split in half
1 clove garlic, minced
1 teaspoon rubbed sage
1/4 teaspoon dried oregano leaves
1/4 teaspoon pepper
   Dash salt
4 slices prosciutto ham
1 tablespoon butter
1 tablespoon olive oil
1/4 cup shredded fresh Parmesan
   cheese
1/2 cup dry white wine
   Fresh sage leaves for garnish

3 to 4 servings

Pound pheasant breasts to 1/4-inch thickness. Sprinkle evenly with garlic, sage, oregano, pepper and salt. Place 1 slice prosciutto on each breast half and secure with wooden pick.

In 12-inch nonstick skillet, heat butter and oil over medium heat. Place breasts prosciutto-side-down in skillet. Cook for 5 to 7 minutes, or until meat is no longer pink, turning breasts over once.

Sprinkle Parmesan cheese evenly over prosciutto. Add wine to skillet. Increase heat to medium-high. Cook for 4 to 5 minutes, or until cheese is melted and wine is nearly boiled away. Remove wooden picks before serving. Garnish with fresh sage leaves.

Per Serving: Calories: 274 • Protein: 30 g. • Carbohydrate: 1 g. • Fat: 15 g.
• Cholesterol: 81 mg. • Sodium: 727 mg.
Exchanges: 4 very lean meat, 3 fat

Pheasant with Sun-dried Tomatoes & Pine Nuts

8 oz. uncooked fettucini
1 tablespoon olive oil
2 whole boneless skinless pheasant breasts (5 to 6 oz. each), cut into 1-inch pieces
3 cloves garlic, minced
2 oz. dry-pack sun-dried tomatoes, rehydrated* and chopped (1 cup)
1 cup heavy whipping cream
1/4 cup snipped fresh basil leaves
1/4 cup pine nuts, toasted**
1/2 teaspoon pepper
   Shredded fresh Parmesan cheese (optional)

3 to 4 servings

Prepare fettucini as directed on package. Drain. Set aside and keep warm. In 12-inch nonstick skillet, heat oil over medium heat. Add pheasant pieces and garlic. Cook for 5 to 6 minutes, or until meat is no longer pink.

Stir in tomatoes, cream, basil, pine nuts and pepper. Cook for 5 to 6 minutes, or until sauce is heated through and slightly thickened, stirring constantly. Add fettucini. Toss to coat. Sprinkle individual servings with Parmesan cheese.

To rehydrate dry-pack sun-dried tomatoes, soak them in hot water for 10 to 15 minutes, or until softened.

**To toast pine nuts, place them in a dry skillet over medium-low heat until lightly browned, shaking pan occasionally.*

Per Serving: Calories: 649 • Protein: 33 g.
• Carbohydrate: 53 g. • Fat: 35 g.
• Cholesterol: 181 mg. • Sodium: 75 mg.
Exchanges: 2¾ starch, 2¾ very lean meat, 2¼ vegetable, 7 fat

Parmesan Pheasant VERY FAST ↑

1/2 cup seasoned dry bread crumbs
1/4 cup shredded fresh Parmesan cheese
2 tablespoons snipped fresh parsley
1 teaspoon garlic powder
1 egg, slightly beaten

4 whole boneless skinless pheasant breasts (5 to 6 oz. each), split in half
3 tablespoons margarine or butter
2 cups prepared chunky marinara sauce
4 slices (1/2 oz. each) Provolone cheese, halved

3 to 4 servings

In shallow baking dish, combine bread crumbs, Parmesan cheese, parsley and garlic powder. Place egg in second shallow dish. Dip pheasant breast halves in egg, then dredge in crumb mixture to coat.

In 10-inch nonstick skillet, melt margarine over medium-high heat. Add breast halves. Cook for 6 to 8 minutes, or until pheasant is golden brown, turning once.

Pour marinara sauce around breast halves in skillet. Top each breast half with 1 slice Provolone. Cover. Cook for 4 to 5 minutes, or until sauce is heated through and cheese is melted.

Per Serving: Calories: 523 • Protein: 50 g. • Carbohydrate: 25 g. • Fat: 25 g.
• Cholesterol: 158 mg. • Sodium: 1590 mg.
Exchanges: ¾ starch, 6 lean meat, 2¾ vegetable, 1½ fat

Pheasant Fajitas

MARINADE:

1/3 cup fresh lime juice
1 teaspoon dried oregano leaves
1 clove garlic, minced
1/2 teaspoon ground cumin
1/2 teaspoon chili powder
1/4 teaspoon sugar
1/4 teaspoon salt
1/4 teaspoon freshly ground pepper

2 whole boneless skinless pheasant breasts (5 to 6 oz. each), cut lengthwise into 1 1/2 × 1/4-inch strips
1 medium onion, thinly sliced
1 medium green pepper, seeded and thinly sliced
8 flour tortillas (8-inch)

GARNISHES (OPTIONAL):
Sour cream
Salsa
Guacamole

4 servings

In medium mixing bowl, combine marinade ingredients. Add pheasant strips, stirring to coat. Cover with plastic wrap. Chill 1 hour. Drain and discard marinade from strips.

Heat 12-inch nonstick skillet over medium-high heat. Spray skillet with nonstick vegetable cooking spray. Add pheasant strips, onion and green pepper. Cook for 4 to 6 minutes, or until meat is no longer pink, stirring frequently. Spoon mixture evenly onto tortillas and serve with desired garnishes.

Per Serving: Calories: 358 • Protein: 26 g. • Carbohydrate: 45 g. • Fat: 8 g. • Cholesterol: 45 mg. • Sodium: 433 mg.
Exchanges: 2 1/2 starch, 2 3/4 very lean meat, 1 vegetable, 1 1/2 fat

Wild Rice-Pheasant Soup ← *LOW-FAT* *FAST*

This very easy recipe is a great way to use cooked pheasant meat and wild rice.

    6 cups ready-to-serve chicken
         broth or water
    3 cups (12 oz.) cut-up cooked
         pheasant (1-inch pieces)
    2 cups cooked wild rice
    2 medium carrots, chopped
         (1 cup)
    2 stalks celery, sliced (1 cup)
  1/3 cup finely chopped onion
    2 cloves garlic, minced
    1 bay leaf
  1/2 teaspoon dried thyme leaves
  1/2 teaspoon salt
  1/2 teaspoon pepper
  1/4 teaspoon snipped fresh parsley

                              8 to 10 cups

In 6-quart Dutch oven or stockpot, combine all ingredients. Bring to a boil over high heat. Cover. Reduce heat to medium-low. Simmer for 20 to 25 minutes, or until vegetables are tender, stirring occasionally. Remove and discard bay leaf before serving.

Per Cup: Calories: 122 • Protein: 13 g.
• Carbohydrate: 9 g. • Fat: 3 g.
• Cholesterol: 30 mg. • Sodium: 742 mg.
Exchanges: 1/2 starch, 1 1/2 very lean meat,
1/2 vegetable, 1/2 fat

Easy Pheasant Pie *FAST*

    1 pkg. (16 oz.) frozen stew
         vegetables (potatoes, carrots,
         onion and celery)
    1 pkg. (.87 oz.) chicken-
         flavored gravy mix
 13/4 cups (7 oz.) chopped cooked
         pheasant
    1 cup frozen peas
    1 teaspoon snipped fresh
         rosemary
         Pastry dough for 2-crust pie*

                              6 servings

Per Serving: Calories: 432 • Protein: 16 g.
• Carbohydrate: 41 g. • Fat: 22 g.
• Cholesterol: 29 mg. • Sodium: 593 mg.
Exchanges: 2 1/4 starch, 1 very lean meat,
1 vegetable, 4 1/4 fat

Heat oven to 425°F. Prepare vegetables as directed on package, cooking just until tender-crisp. Drain. Set aside. Prepare gravy mix as directed on package. Add pheasant, peas and rosemary to gravy. Set aside.

On lightly floured surface, roll half of pastry dough into 12-inch circle. Fit circle into 9-inch pie plate. Spread vegetables in bottom of crust. Top with pheasant mixture. Roll remaining dough into 11-inch circle. Cut vents in circle with sharp knife. Place circle over top of pie. Roll edges of bottom and top crusts together. Flute edges or press together with tines of fork to seal.

Bake for 15 minutes. Reduce heat to 400°F. Bake for 15 to 20 minutes longer, or until filling is bubbly and crust is browned. Let stand for 10 minutes before serving.

*Use your favorite crust recipe or 1 pkg. (15 oz.) refrigerated pie crust dough.

White Pheasant Pizza with Roasted Red Pepper

This is a terrific way to use leftover cooked pheasant meat or any game bird meat. An Alfredo-like sauce, roasted peppers and capers give it an elegant touch and delicate flavor.

SAUCE:

- 1 tablespoon butter or margarine
- 1/4 cup finely chopped onion
- 2 cloves garlic, minced
- 1 tablespoon plus 1 teaspoon all-purpose flour
- 1/8 teaspoon white pepper
- 1 cup 2% milk
- 1/4 teaspoon instant chicken bouillon granules
- 1/3 cup shredded fresh Parmesan cheese

- 1 prepared pizza crust (12-inch)
- 1 small onion, thinly sliced
- 1 1/2 cups (6 oz.) cut-up cooked pheasant (1-inch pieces)
- 1 medium red pepper, roasted*, seeded and cut into strips
- 1 cup (4 oz.) shredded Monterey Jack cheese
- 1 tablespoon capers, drained

6 servings

Heat oven to 425°F. In 1-quart saucepan, melt butter over medium-low heat. Add chopped onion and the garlic. Cook for 2 to 3 minutes, or until onion is tender, stirring frequently. Stir in flour and white pepper. Blend in milk and bouillon. Cook for 8 to 10 minutes, or until sauce is thickened and bubbly, stirring constantly. Remove from heat. Add Parmesan cheese. Stir until melted.

Place crust on pizza pan, pizza stone or baking sheet. Spread sauce to within 1 inch of edge. Top sauce evenly with sliced onion, pheasant pieces, red pepper and cheese. Bake for 15 to 18 minutes, or until cheese is melted and lightly browned. Sprinkle with capers.

To roast red pepper, place it under broiler with surface 4 inches from heat. Roast until skin is blackened and blistered, turning pepper frequently. Place pepper in closed paper or plastic bag for 10 minutes. Peel and discard skin from pepper; prepare as directed.

Per Serving: Calories: 324 • Protein: 22 g. • Carbohydrate: 29 g. • Fat: 13 g.
• Cholesterol: 58 mg. • Sodium: 622 mg.
Exchanges: 1¾ starch, 2¼ lean meat, ½ vegetable, 1¼ fat

Cranberry-Pheasant Wild Rice Salad

Sugared cranberries and almonds add a delicious sweet and tangy dimension to this hearty salad.

3 cups cooked wild rice
2 cups (8 oz.) cubed cooked pheasant (¾-inch cubes)
1 cup sliced celery
1 cup sliced almonds
1 pkg. (12 oz.) fresh or frozen cranberries
⅔ cup sugar

DRESSING:
¼ cup vegetable oil
3 tablespoons frozen orange juice concentrate, defrosted
3 tablespoons red wine vinegar
2 tablespoons sugar
2 teaspoons grated fresh orange peel
¼ teaspoon salt

4 to 6 servings

Heat oven to 350°F. In large salad bowl or mixing bowl, combine rice, pheasant and celery. Set aside.

Spread almonds in single layer on 15½ × 10½-inch baking sheet with edges. Bake for 2 to 3 minutes, or until golden brown. Add cranberries. Sprinkle evenly with ⅔ cup sugar. Stir to coat almonds and cranberries with sugar. Spread mixture evenly on baking sheet. Bake for 8 to 10 minutes, or until sugar melts and cranberries are glazed, stirring occasionally. Cool slightly and stir into wild rice mixture.

In 1-cup measure, combine all dressing ingredients. Mix well. Pour dressing over salad, tossing to coat. Chill before serving.

Per Serving: Calories: 472 • Protein: 19 g. • Carbohydrate: 59 g. • Fat: 19 g. • Cholesterol: 33 mg. • Sodium: 131 mg.
Exchanges: 1½ starch, 2 very lean meat, ½ fruit, 4 fat

Marinated Pheasant Salad

This is a full-meal salad that makes a nice lunch or light dinner entrée.

2½ cups (10 oz.) shredded cooked pheasant
1 can (14 oz.) quartered artichoke hearts, drained
½ medium red onion, cut into very thin wedges and separated (½ cup)
½ cup Italian dressing
8 cups torn mixed baby salad greens
2 Roma tomatoes, sliced
½ cup pitted halved Kalamata olives
½ cup (2 oz.) crumbled blue cheese

4 to 6 servings

In medium mixing bowl, combine pheasant, artichoke hearts, onion and dressing. Toss to coat. Cover with plastic wrap. Chill at least 2 hours, stirring occasionally.

In large salad bowl or mixing bowl, combine greens, tomatoes and olives. Add pheasant mixture. Toss to combine. Sprinkle cheese over top of salad.

Per Serving: Calories: 279 • Protein: 20 g. • Carbohydrate: 11 g. • Fat: 18 g. • Cholesterol: 49 mg. • Sodium: 534 mg. Exchanges: 2¼ very lean meat, 2 vegetable, 3½ fat

Light–Medium Birds

Menu

Chukar Partridge with Pears (recipe below) ❧ *Herbed Focaccia (recipe below)*
Roasted New Potatoes ❧ *Steamed Snow Pea Pods, Broccoli or Asparagus*

Chukar Partridge with Pears

8 small red pears*, halved and
   cored
2 whole dressed chukar
   partridges (3/4 to 1 lb. each),
   skin on, halved
2 cups water
2 tablespoons fresh lemon juice
1/2 cup tawny port
1/2 cup pear nectar
2 tablespoons butter
1 tablespoon packed brown sugar
1/2 teaspoon lemon peel

4 servings

Per Serving: Calories: 478 • Protein: 40 g.
• Carbohydrate: 30 g. • Fat: 22 g.
• Cholesterol: 137 mg. • Sodium: 132 mg.
Exchanges: 5½ lean meat, 1½ fruit,
1¼ fat

Heat oven to 350°F. Cut 4 pear halves in half again. Place 2 pieces of pear in cavity of each partridge half. In large mixing bowl, combine remaining pears, the water and juice. Set aside.

Arrange partridge halves skin-side-up in 13 × 9-inch roasting pan. Add port and nectar to pan. Roast partridges for 30 to 45 minutes, or until meat is tender, basting partridges occasionally. Remove from oven. Heat broiler. Place partridge halves under broiler with surface of partridges 6 inches from heat. Broil for 5 to 7 minutes, or until partridges are browned.

Meanwhile, in 12-inch nonstick skillet, melt butter over medium heat. Drain water mixture from remaining pears and pat pears dry with paper towels. Add pears to skillet. Cook for 5 to 7 minutes, or until pears are golden brown, stirring occasionally. Remove from heat. Sprinkle pears evenly with sugar and peel. Serve sugared pears with partridges.

Seckel pears are preferred, but if they are unavailable, use 4 medium red pears. Cut 1 into eighths and 3 into quarters. Use the eighths to stuff the partridge halves.

Herbed Focaccia

1 cup warm water (105° to
   115°F)
1 tablespoon active dry yeast
2 tablespoons olive oil
1 tablespoon dried herb leaves
   (oregano, basil or rosemary,
   or a combination)
1 teaspoon salt
3½ cups all-purpose flour,
   divided
2 to 3 teaspoons yellow
   cornmeal

4 to 6 servings

Per Serving: Calories: 331 • Protein: 9 g.
• Carbohydrate: 60 g. • Fat: 6 g.
• Cholesterol: 0 mg. • Sodium: 369 mg.
Exchanges: 3½ starch, 1 fat

In large mixing bowl, combine water and yeast. Let stand for 5 minutes to dissolve yeast. Stir in oil, herbs and salt. Stir in 2 cups flour. Beat well with wooden spoon. Gradually add enough of remaining flour to form a soft dough that pulls away from sides of bowl.

Turn dough out onto lightly floured surface. Knead for 8 to 10 minutes, or until dough is smooth and elastic, adding flour as necessary to prevent stickiness. Spray medium mixing bowl with nonstick vegetable cooking spray. Place dough in bowl, turning to coat dough. Spray piece of plastic wrap with nonstick vegetable cooking spray. Place wrap loosely over bowl. Let dough rise in warm, draft-free place for 1 to 1¼ hours, or until dough is doubled in size.

Heat oven to 375°F. Spray baking sheet with nonstick vegetable cooking spray. Sprinkle baking sheet evenly with cornmeal. Punch down dough. On lightly floured surface, knead dough briefly, then press into 11-inch circle. Place dough circle on prepared baking sheet. Let rest in warm, draft-free place for 20 minutes. Using fingertips, poke dough randomly at 2-inch intervals. Bake for 20 to 25 minutes, or until golden brown.

TIP: Just before baking, brush surface of dough with olive oil and sprinkle lightly with kosher salt.

Orange Ruffed Grouse

- 1 medium orange, unpeeled, quartered
- 2 whole dressed ruffed grouse (¾ to 1 lb. each), skin removed
  Salt and pepper to taste
- 2 strips bacon, halved
- ½ cup frozen orange juice concentrate, defrosted
- ¼ cup ready-to-serve chicken broth or water
- ¼ teaspoon dried thyme leaves

4 servings

Heat oven to 350°F. Stuff 2 orange wedges into cavity of each grouse. Salt and pepper surface of grouse to taste. Lay bacon strips evenly over grouse. Arrange grouse in 13 × 9-inch roasting pan.

In 1-cup measure, combine concentrate, broth and thyme. Pour ½ cup sauce over grouse. Roast grouse for 40 to 50 minutes, or until meat is tender and grouse are browned, basting occasionally with remaining sauce.

Per Serving: Calories: 340 • Protein: 38 g.
• Carbohydrate: 20 g. • Fat: 12 g.
• Cholesterol: 108 mg.
• Sodium: 198 mg.
Exchanges:
5 very lean meat,
1¼ fruit, 2½ fat

Apple-Ginger Ruffed Grouse LOW-FAT ↓

- 1 tablespoon butter or margarine
- 2 whole dressed ruffed grouse (¾ to 1 lb. each), skin removed, quartered
- 1 can (14½ oz.) ready-to-serve chicken broth
- 1 medium onion, sliced
- 2 teaspoons grated fresh gingerroot
- 1 stick cinnamon (3 inches long)
- ½ teaspoon salt
- ¼ teaspoon pepper
- 2 red cooking apples, cored and sliced
- 1 tablespoon cornstarch mixed with 2 tablespoons water

4 servings

In 12-inch nonstick skillet, melt butter over medium heat. Add grouse pieces. Cook for 5 to 7 minutes, or until browned, turning grouse occasionally. Add broth, onion, gingerroot, cinnamon, salt and pepper. Bring to a simmer. Cover. Reduce heat to low. Simmer for 20 minutes.

Add apple slices to skillet. Re-cover. Simmer for 10 to 15 minutes, or until meat is tender. Remove grouse, apples and onion from skillet, and arrange on warm serving platter. Set aside and keep warm.

Whisk cornstarch mixture into pan juices. Bring to a boil over medium-high heat. Boil for 1 minute, stirring constantly. Spoon sauce over grouse.

Per Serving: Calories: 299 • Protein: 37 g. • Carbohydrate: 14 g. • Fat: 10 g.
• Cholesterol: 108 mg. • Sodium: 798 mg.
Exchanges: 5 very lean meat, 1 vegetable, ½ fruit, 2 fat

Raspberry-Sherry Glazed Ruffed Grouse ⏱ VERY FAST ↓

4 whole boneless, skinless ruffed grouse breasts
   (4 to 6 oz. each), split in half, pounded to
   ¼-inch thickness
¼ teaspoon salt
2 tablespoons butter or margarine
¼ cup finely chopped red onion
2 tablespoons raspberry vinegar
¼ cup ready-to-serve chicken broth
2 tablespoons cream sherry
¼ cup heavy whipping cream
   Fresh raspberries (optional)

4 servings

Sprinkle grouse breasts evenly with salt. In 12-inch
nonstick skillet, melt butter over medium heat. Add
breasts. Cook breasts for 2 to 4 minutes, or until
lightly browned, turning breasts over once. Remove
from skillet. Set aside and keep warm.

Add onion to skillet. Reduce heat to low. Cook for 3
to 4 minutes, or until onion is tender, stirring occasionally. Stir in vinegar. Increase heat to medium.
Simmer for 3 to 4 minutes, or until liquid is
reduced by half, stirring occasionally. Stir in
broth and sherry. Simmer for 1 minute.

Return grouse breasts to skillet. Reduce
heat to low. Simmer for 5 to 7 minutes,
or until meat is desired doneness,
basting breasts frequently.
Remove from heat. Stir in
cream. Serve grouse breasts
with sauce. Garnish with
fresh raspberries.

Per Serving: Calories: 309
• Protein: 35 g.
• Carbohydrate: 2 g.
• Fat: 16 g.
• Cholesterol: 118 mg.
• Sodium: 310 mg.
Exchanges: 5 very
lean meat, 3¼ fat

Lemon-Honey Ruffed Grouse ◁LOW-FAT▷

   Salt and pepper to taste
2 whole dressed ruffed grouse (¾ to 1 lb. each),
   skin removed

GLAZE:
⅓ cup honey
½ teaspoon grated lemon peel
3 tablespoons fresh lemon juice
⅛ teaspoon ground allspice

4 servings

Heat oven to 350°F. Salt and pepper grouse to taste.
Arrange grouse in 13 × 9-inch roasting pan. Cover
with foil. Roast for 20 minutes. Meanwhile, in 1-cup
measure, combine glaze ingredients.

Remove foil. Brush grouse with glaze. Roast for
25 to 35 minutes, or until golden brown, basting
occasionally with glaze.

Per Serving: Calories: 290 • Protein: 36 g. • Carbohydrate: 24 g.
• Fat: 6 g. • Cholesterol: 100 mg. • Sodium: 58 mg.
Exchanges: 5 very lean meat, 1 fat

Creamy Ruffed Grouse with Rosemary

2 tablespoons butter or margarine
2 whole dressed ruffed grouse (¾ to 1 lb. each), skin removed, halved
Salt and pepper to taste
8 oz. fresh mushrooms, sliced (3 cups)
⅓ cup chopped onion
1 teaspoon dried rosemary, crushed
1½ cups sour cream
⅓ cup ready-to-serve chicken broth
3 tablespoons all-purpose flour
1 teaspoon Worcestershire sauce
¼ teaspoon freshly ground pepper
Snipped fresh parsley (optional)

4 servings

Heat oven to 350°F. In 12-inch nonstick skillet, melt butter over medium heat. Add grouse halves. Cook for 5 to 7 minutes, or until browned, turning grouse occasionally.

Spray 12 × 8-inch baking dish with nonstick vegetable cooking spray. Arrange grouse halves in dish. Season to taste with salt and pepper. Set aside.

Add mushrooms, onion and rosemary to drippings in skillet. Cook over medium heat for 3 to 5 minutes, or until vegetables are tender, stirring occasionally. Remove from heat. In medium mixing bowl, combine sour cream, broth, flour, Worcestershire sauce and ¼ teaspoon pepper. Stir sour cream mixture into skillet. Spoon mixture over grouse. Cover dish with foil.

Bake for 1 to 1¼ hours, or until meat is tender. Garnish with snipped fresh parsley.

Per Serving: Calories: 485 • Protein: 41 g. • Carbohydrate: 12 g. • Fat: 30 g. • Cholesterol: 154 mg. • Sodium: 260 mg.
Exchanges: ¼ starch, 5 very lean meat, 1¾ vegetable, 6 fat

Ruffed Grouse Fruit Salad →

- 4 cups mixed salad greens
- 1 can (11 oz.) mandarin oranges, drained
- 1 small red onion, thinly sliced
- 2 kiwifruit, peeled and sliced
- ¾ cup fresh raspberries or pomegranate seeds
- ⅓ cup pecan halves, toasted
- ⅓ cup vegetable oil
- 3 tablespoons raspberry vinegar
- 1½ tablespoons sugar
- ¼ teaspoon salt
  Dash red pepper sauce
- 4 whole boneless skinless ruffed grouse breasts (4 to 6 oz. each), split in half

4 servings

Prepare grill for medium direct heat. On individual serving plates, evenly arrange greens, oranges, onion, kiwifruit, raspberries and pecans. Set aside. In 1-quart saucepan, combine oil, vinegar, sugar, salt and red pepper sauce. Bring to a boil over medium-high heat, stirring frequently. Set dressing aside and keep warm.

Spray cooking grid with nonstick vegetable cooking spray. Arrange grouse breasts on cooking grid. Grill for 8 to 10 minutes, or until meat is no longer pink and juices run clear. Place 2 breast halves on each prepared plate. Drizzle warm dressing evenly over salads. Serve immediately.

Per Serving: Calories: 536 • Protein: 38 g. • Carbohydrate: 33 g. • Fat: 29 g. • Cholesterol: 82 mg. • Sodium: 209 mg. Exchanges: 5 very lean meat, 2 vegetable, 1½ fruit, 5½ fat

Ruffed Grouse with Chestnuts & Cranberries

- 4 oz. whole fresh chestnuts
- 2 tablespoons butter or margarine
- 12 oz. boneless skinless ruffed grouse meat, cut into 1-inch cubes
- 4 stalks celery, sliced (2 cups)
- ½ cup chopped shallots
- 2 cloves garlic, minced
- ⅓ cup ready-to-serve chicken broth
- ½ teaspoon dried thyme leaves
- ½ cup fresh cranberries
- 4 cups hot cooked Basmati rice

4 servings

To remove shells from chestnuts, first cut a small strip of shell from each nut. Place chestnuts in 1-quart saucepan. Add water to just cover chestnuts. Bring to a boil over high heat. Boil for 2 minutes. Drain. Cool slightly. Using sharp knife, peel shell and skin off chestnuts. Chop chestnuts. Set aside.

In 12-inch nonstick skillet, melt butter over medium-high heat. Add grouse. Cook for 4 to 5 minutes, or until meat is lightly browned, stirring frequently. Add chestnuts, celery, shallots and garlic. Cook for 3 to 4 minutes, or until celery is tender-crisp, stirring frequently. Add broth and thyme. Bring to a boil. Cover. Reduce heat to medium-low. Simmer for 4 to 5 minutes, or until grouse is tender.

Stir in cranberries. Cook, uncovered, for 1 to 3 minutes, or until cranberries just begin to pop, stirring frequently. Serve over rice.

Per Serving: Calories: 450 • Protein: 29 g. • Carbohydrate: 66 g. • Fat: 10 g. • Cholesterol: 65 mg. • Sodium: 252 mg. Exchanges: 3½ starch, 2¼ very lean meat, 1 vegetable, 2 fat

Blue Grouse Madeira with Chutney ↓

2 whole dressed blue grouse
   (1 to 2¼ lbs. each), skin on, quartered
⅓ cup Madeira wine
   Salt and pepper to taste
¼ cup chopped shallots
1 clove garlic, minced
4 to 6 cups hot cooked wild and white rice
   blend
4 to 6 tablespoons prepared chutney

4 to 6 servings

Heat oven to 350°F. Spray 13 × 9-inch baking dish with nonstick vegetable cooking spray. Arrange grouse pieces skin-side-up in dish. Pour wine over grouse. Season to taste with salt and pepper. Sprinkle shallots and garlic evenly over grouse. Cover with foil.

Bake for 50 minutes. Remove foil. Baste grouse with pan juices. Bake, uncovered, for 10 to 15 minutes longer, or until grouse pieces are lightly browned. Serve grouse over rice with chutney on the side.

Per Serving: Calories: 568 • Protein: 50 g. • Carbohydrate: 49 g. • Fat: 19 g. • Cholesterol: 139 mg. • Sodium: 646 mg.
Exchanges: 2¼ starch, 6¼ lean meat

Minted Blue Grouse

2 tablespoons butter or margarine
2 whole dressed blue grouse (1 to 2¼ lbs. each),
   skin on, quartered
1 teaspoon salt
½ teaspoon pepper
1 small onion, sliced
½ cup apple-mint jelly
½ cup dry white wine
¼ cup chopped shallots

4 to 6 servings

Heat oven to 350°F. Spray 13 × 9-inch baking dish with nonstick vegetable cooking spray. Set aside. In 12-inch nonstick skillet, melt butter over medium heat. Add grouse pieces. Cook for 5 to 7 minutes, or until browned, turning grouse occasionally.

Arrange grouse skin-side-up in prepared dish. Sprinkle evenly with salt and pepper. Set aside. Add onion, jelly, wine and shallots to skillet. Cook over medium heat for 2 to 3 minutes, or until jelly melts and is smooth, stirring constantly. Spoon mixture over grouse. Cover with foil.

Bake for 1 to 1¼ hours, or until meat is tender. Serve grouse with sauce from dish.

Per Serving: Calories: 469 • Protein: 45 g. • Carbohydrate: 21 g. • Fat: 22 g. • Cholesterol: 149 mg. • Sodium: 495 mg.
Exchanges: 6¼ lean meat, ½ vegetable, ¾ fat

Fennel-braised Blue Grouse

This recipe is a good way to prepare an older, tougher bird.

   1 whole dressed blue grouse (1 to 2¼ lbs.),
        skin on, halved
      Salt and pepper to taste
⅓ cup all-purpose flour
   2 tablespoons olive oil
   2 tablespoons butter or margarine
¼ cup finely chopped shallots
   6 whole cloves garlic, peeled
   1 medium onion, sliced
   1 can (14½ oz.) diced tomatoes, drained
   1 cup ready-to-serve chicken broth
   1 cup orange juice
   1 tablespoon apple cider vinegar
½ teaspoon dried thyme leaves
   1 medium fennel bulb, peeled and cut into wedges

2 to 3 servings

Heat oven to 350°F. Season grouse halves with salt and pepper to taste. Dredge in flour to coat. In 12-inch skillet, heat oil and butter over medium heat. Add grouse. Cook for 5 to 7 minutes, or until browned, turning grouse occasionally. Remove grouse from skillet and set aside.

Add shallots and garlic to skillet. Cook for 2 to 3 minutes, or until garlic is soft but not browned, stirring frequently. Add onion. Cook for 5 to 6 minutes, or until onion is tender, stirring frequently. Stir in tomatoes, broth, juice, vinegar and thyme. Bring to a simmer over medium-high heat.

Spoon onion mixture into 10-inch square casserole. Arrange grouse halves skin-side-up over mixture. Arrange fennel around grouse. Cover. Bake for 1 to 1½ hours, or until meat is tender.

Per Serving: Calories: 684 • Protein: 51 g. • Carbohydrate: 38 g.
• Fat: 36 g. • Cholesterol: 159 mg. • Sodium: 820 mg.
Exchanges: ¾ starch, 6¼ lean meat, 2¾ vegetable, ¾ fruit, 3½ fat

Lemon-Rosemary Chukar Partridge ↑

   2 whole dressed chukar partridges (¾ to 1 lb.
        each), skin on, halved
   8 thin slices lemon
   1 teaspoon dried rosemary leaves
¼ teaspoon salt
¼ teaspoon pepper
   2 tablespoons water
   2 tablespoons fresh lemon juice

4 servings

Heat oven to 350°F. Loosen skin on breasts of partridges. Place 1 lemon slice under skin of each partridge half. Spray 13 × 9-inch baking pan with nonstick vegetable cooking spray. Arrange partridge halves skin-side-up in pan. Sprinkle evenly with rosemary, salt and pepper. Arrange remaining 4 lemon slices over partridges.

In small bowl, combine water and juice. Pour mixture into pan. Cover pan with foil. Bake for 20 to 25 minutes, or until meat is tender. Remove pan from oven. Remove foil. Heat broiler. Place partridge halves under broiler with surface of partridges 4 to 5 inches from heat. Broil for 2 to 3 minutes, or until partridges are lightly browned.

Per Serving: Calories: 317 • Protein: 39 g. • Carbohydrate: 2 g.
• Fat: 16 g. • Cholesterol: 122 mg. • Sodium: 206 mg.
Exchanges: 5½ lean meat

Sweet & Hot Glazed Chukars

MARINADE:

  2 fresh hot red chili peppers, seeded and chopped*

½ cup sugar

½ cup rice wine vinegar

½ cup raisins

  3 cloves garlic, minced

  1 teaspoon salt

½ teaspoon grated fresh gingerroot

¼ cup vegetable oil

  2 whole dressed chukar partridges (¾ to 1 lb. each), skin on, halved

4 servings

In 1-quart saucepan, combine all marinade ingredients, except oil. Bring to a boil over medium-high heat. Reduce heat to medium-low. Simmer for 10 minutes to plump raisins and blend flavors, stirring occasionally. Remove from heat and cool completely. Add oil to marinade, whisking well to blend.

Arrange partridge halves in shallow dish. Pour marinade over partridges, turning to coat. Cover with plastic wrap. Chill several hours or overnight, turning partridge halves occasionally.

Prepare grill for medium-direct heat. Spray cooking grid with nonstick vegetable cooking spray. Drain and reserve marinade from partridges. Place marinade in 1-quart saucepan and bring to a boil over medium-high heat. Remove from heat. Set aside and keep warm.

Arrange partridge halves on cooking grid. Grill, covered, for 15 to 20 minutes, or until meat is tender, turning partridges and basting occasionally with reserved marinade. Serve any remaining marinade with partridges.

*Be careful when chopping hot chilies. Wear rubber gloves and do not touch face or eyes while working with chilies.

Per Serving: Calories: 592 • Protein: 40 g. • Carbohydrate: 42 g. • Fat: 30 g. • Cholesterol: 122 mg. • Sodium: 622 mg.
Exchanges: 5½ lean meat, 1 fruit, 2½ fat

Chukar Partridge in Rosemary-Cream Sauce

- ⅓ cup plus 2 tablespoons all-purpose flour, divided
- ¼ teaspoon salt
- ¼ teaspoon freshly ground pepper
- 2 whole dressed chukar partridges (¾ to 1 lb. each), skin removed, halved
- ⅓ cup vegetable oil
- 2 medium russet potatoes, cut into ½-inch cubes
- 2 medium carrots, cut into 1-inch pieces
- 1 cup quartered fresh mushrooms
- ½ cup halved pearl onions
- 2 tablespoons butter or margarine
- 1⅓ cups half-and-half
- ⅓ cup cream sherry
- ¼ cup dry white wine
- ½ teaspoon dried rosemary leaves

4 servings

Heat oven to 350°F. In shallow dish, combine ⅓ cup flour, the salt and pepper. Dredge partridge halves in flour mixture to coat. In 12-inch skillet, heat oil over medium-high heat. Add partridges. Cook for 3 to 4 minutes, or until browned, turning partridges occasionally. Drain partridges on paper-towel-lined plate.

Arrange partridge halves in 13 × 9-inch baking dish. Arrange potatoes, carrots, mushrooms and onions around partridges. Set aside.

In 1-quart saucepan, melt butter over low heat. Stir in remaining 2 tablespoons flour. Cook for 1 minute, stirring constantly. Gradually stir in half-and-half. Stir until smooth. Stir in sherry, wine and rosemary. Pour cream sauce over partridges. Cover with foil. Bake for 1 to 1¼ hours, or until meat is tender and vegetables are tender-crisp.

Per Serving: Calories: 675 • Protein: 42 g. • Carbohydrate: 39 g. • Fat: 39 g. • Cholesterol: 145 mg. • Sodium: 308 mg. Exchanges: 1½ starch, 5 very lean meat, 2 vegetable, 7½ fat

Apple Cider Partridge ↓

- ¼ cup all-purpose flour
- ½ teaspoon ground ginger
- ¼ teaspoon ground cinnamon
- 2 whole dressed chukar partridges (¾ to 1 lb. each), skin removed, halved
- 2 tablespoons vegetable oil
- 1½ cups apple cider
- ¼ cup applejack liqueur
- 3 tablespoons packed brown sugar
- 2 red cooking apples, cored and thinly sliced
- 1½ teaspoons cornstarch mixed with 2 tablespoons water

4 servings

In shallow dish, combine flour, ginger and cinnamon. Dredge partridge halves in flour mixture to coat. In 12-inch nonstick skillet, heat oil over medium-high heat. Add partridges. Cook for 5 to 7 minutes, or until browned, turning partridges occasionally.

Meanwhile, in 2-cup measure, combine cider, applejack and sugar. When partridge halves are browned, pour mixture into skillet. Bring to a boil. Reduce heat to low. Cover. Simmer for 15 to 18 minutes, or until meat is tender.

Add apple slices to skillet. Cover and simmer for 2 to 3 minutes, or until apples are tender. Stir in cornstarch mixture. Cook for 1 to 2 minutes, or until liquid is thickened and glossy, stirring constantly.

Per Serving: Calories: 429 • Protein: 37 g. • Carbohydrate: 41 g. • Fat: 13 g • Cholesterol: 100 mg. • Sodium: 63 mg. Exchanges: ½ starch, 5 very lean meat, 1¼ fruit, 2½ fat

Herb & Cheese Stuffed Chukar Breasts

4 whole boneless skinless chukar
  partridge breasts (4 to 6 oz.
  each), split in half
  Salt and pepper to taste
3 tablespoons butter, softened
1 tablespoon snipped fresh
  parsley
½ teaspoon dried oregano leaves,
  crushed
½ teaspoon dried marjoram
  leaves, crushed
⅛ teaspoon ground nutmeg
2 oz. Bel Paese cheese* or fresh
  mozzarella, cut into 4 slices
¼ cup all-purpose flour
1 egg, lightly beaten
⅓ cup unseasoned dry bread
  crumbs
2 tablespoons vegetable oil
½ cup dry white wine

4 servings

Pound breast halves to ¼-inch thickness. Season to taste with salt and pepper. Set aside.

In small bowl, combine butter, parsley, oregano, marjoram and nutmeg. Place 1 slice cheese on each of 4 breast halves. Top cheese slices evenly with half of butter mixture. Top each with one of remaining 4 breast halves. Secure with wooden picks.

Place flour, egg and crumbs in 3 separate, shallow dishes. Dredge stuffed breasts in flour, then dip in egg and dredge in crumbs to coat. In 12-inch nonstick skillet, heat oil over medium heat. Add stuffed breasts. Cook for 7 to 9 minutes, or until meat is desired doneness, turning breasts over once or twice. Add wine to skillet. Simmer for 3 to 4 minutes, or until wine is nearly reduced, turning breasts over once. Place breasts on serving platter. Set aside and keep warm.

Wipe out skillet. In same skillet, melt remaining butter mixture over medium heat. Spoon mixture over partridge breasts.

Bel Paese cheese is a semisoft Italian cheese with a mild, buttery flavor. Its name means "beautiful country."

Per Serving: Calories: 484 • Protein: 42 g. • Carbohydrate: 13 g. • Fat: 26 g.
• Cholesterol: 175 mg. • Sodium: 343 mg.
Exchanges: ¾ starch, 5½ very lean meat, 5 fat

Grill-smoked Chukar Partridge

MARINADE:

¼ cup balsamic vinegar
2 teaspoons dried oregano leaves
2 teaspoons Worcestershire sauce
1 teaspoon dried rubbed sage
1 clove garlic, minced
½ teaspoon dried thyme leaves
½ teaspoon sugar
½ teaspoon salt
 Dash ground nutmeg
1 cup olive oil
2 whole dressed chukar partridges (¾ to 1 lb. each), skin on, halved
 Apple wood chips

4 servings

In food processor or blender, combine all marinade ingredients, except oil. Process until blended. With processor running, gradually add oil in slow drizzle until well blended. In shallow dish or sealable bag, combine partridge halves and marinade. Turn partridges to coat. Cover dish with plastic wrap, or seal bag. Refrigerate several hours or overnight, turning partridges occasionally.

Soak wood chips in warm water for 30 minutes; drain. Prepare grill for medium direct heat. Spray cooking grid with nonstick vegetable cooking spray. Drain and discard marinade from partridges. Sprinkle a handful of wood chips over charcoal in grill. Cover grill until chips begin to smoke.

Arrange partridge halves on cooking grid. Grill, covered, for 15 to 20 minutes, or until meat is tender, turning partridges occasionally.

Per Serving: Calories: 435 • Protein: 39 g.
• Carbohydrate: 1 g. • Fat: 29 g.
• Cholesterol: 122 mg. • Sodium: 218 mg.
Exchanges: 5½ lean meat, 2½ fat

Sautéed Ruffed Grouse with Thyme LOW-FAT ↑

1 tablespoon butter or margarine
2 whole dressed ruffed grouse (¾ to 1 lb. each), skin removed, quartered
1 tablespoon snipped fresh thyme
½ teaspoon salt
½ teaspoon pepper
¼ teaspoon garlic powder

4 servings

In 12-inch nonstick skillet, melt butter over medium heat. Add grouse pieces. Cook for 5 to 7 minutes, or until browned, turning grouse pieces once or twice.

Reduce heat to low. Sprinkle thyme, salt, pepper and garlic powder evenly over grouse. Cover. Cook for 20 to 25 minutes, or until meat is tender, turning grouse over occasionally.

Per Serving: Calories: 230 • Protein: 36 g. • Carbohydrate: <1 g. • Fat: 8 g.
• Cholesterol: 108 mg. • Sodium: 359 mg.
Exchanges: 5 very lean meat, 1½ fat

Risotto Grouse Casserole

1 oz. dried porcini mushrooms, coarsely chopped, rinsed

1 cup hot water

4 tablespoons butter, divided

3 medium carrots, finely chopped (1⅓ cups)

½ cup thinly sliced green onions

2 cups uncooked arborio rice

3 cups hot ready-to-serve chicken broth, divided

½ cup dry white wine

8 oz. boneless skinless blue grouse meat, cut into ½-inch cubes

3 cloves garlic, minced

½ cup snipped fresh parsley
Salt and pepper to taste

2 cups shredded fresh Parmesan cheese, divided

1 cup half-and-half

2 eggs
Pinch ground nutmeg

4 to 6 servings

Heat oven to 350°F. Spray 2-quart casserole with nonstick vegetable cooking spray. Set aside. In small mixing bowl, combine mushrooms and water. Set aside for 30 minutes.

In 12-inch nonstick skillet, melt 3 tablespoons butter over medium heat. Add carrots and onions. Cook for 6 to 7 minutes, or until tender, stirring constantly. Stir in rice. Cook for 1 minute, stirring constantly. Drain liquid from mushrooms. Set mushrooms aside. Add mushroom liquid to skillet. Add 2 cups broth and the wine to skillet. Bring to a simmer. Cover. Reduce heat to low. Simmer for 30 to 40 minutes, or until rice is tender but firm, adding remaining broth as liquid in skillet is absorbed and stirring occasionally.

Meanwhile, in 10-inch nonstick skillet, melt remaining 1 tablespoon butter over medium heat. Add grouse, garlic and mushrooms. Cook for 3 to 4 minutes, or until meat is no longer pink, stirring frequently. Stir in parsley. Cook for 1 minute, stirring frequently. Stir in salt and pepper to taste. Remove from heat.

Spread half of rice mixture in prepared dish. Top with grouse mixture, 1 cup Parmesan cheese and remaining rice mixture. In medium mixing bowl, whisk together half-and-half, eggs and nutmeg. Pour over rice mixture. Top with remaining 1 cup Parmesan cheese. Bake for 40 to 50 minutes, or until top is puffed and lightly browned. Let stand for 5 minutes before serving.

Per Serving: Calories: 629 • Protein: 32 g. • Carbohydrate: 63 g. • Fat: 27 g. • Cholesterol: 157 mg. • Sodium: 1251 mg.
Exchanges: 3½ starch, 2¾ medium-fat meat, 1¼ vegetable, 2½ fat

Chukar Partridge with Lentils

1½ cups water
⅔ cup uncooked brown lentils, rinsed and sorted
1 small onion, quartered
1 medium carrot, halved
1 clove garlic, crushed
1 sprig fresh parsley
2 whole dressed chukar partridges (¾ to 1 lb. each), skin on
    Salt and pepper to taste
2 tablespoons butter or margarine
1 small onion, chopped (½ cup)
1 medium carrot, sliced (½ cup)
½ cup dry white wine
½ cup ready-to-serve chicken broth

4 servings

In 1-quart saucepan, combine water, lentils, quartered onion, halved carrot, garlic and parsley. Bring to a boil over medium-high heat. Cover. Reduce heat to medium-low. Simmer for 30 to 35 minutes, or until lentils are tender. Drain and discard excess liquid. Remove and discard onion, carrot, garlic and parsley. Set lentils aside and keep warm.

Meanwhile, season surface and cavities of partridges to taste with salt and pepper. Tuck wings behind backs and truss legs of partridges. Set aside. In 12-inch nonstick skillet, melt butter over medium heat. Add chopped onion and sliced carrot. Cook for 4 to 5 minutes, or until onion is tender. Increase heat to medium-high. Add partridges. Cook for 5 to 6 minutes, or until partridges are browned, turning frequently.

Add wine and broth to skillet, stirring to loosen any browned bits from pan. Reduce heat to medium-low. Arrange partridges breast-side-down. Cover. Simmer for 14 to 16 minutes, or until meat is tender.

Spread lentils on serving platter. Arrange partridges on lentils. Set aside and keep warm. Bring liquid in skillet to a boil over medium-high heat. Boil for 5 to 7 minutes, or until liquid is reduced by two-thirds. Spoon sauce over partridges and lentils.

Per Serving: Calories: 527 • Protein: 49 g. • Carbohydrate: 26 g. • Fat: 22 g.
• Cholesterol: 137 mg. • Sodium: 270 mg.
Exchanges: 1½ starch, 5½ lean meat, ¾ vegetable, 1¼ fat

Dark–Medium Birds

Menu

Billy's Spicy Oriental Sharptail (recipe below)
Cucumber-Yogurt Salad (recipe below) ❧ *Flatbread*

Billy's Spicy Oriental Sharptail ⟨LOW-FAT⟩

MARINADE:
½ cup soy sauce (regular or low-
     sodium)
½ cup brandy or Cognac
½ cup chopped dried figs
⅓ cup chopped shallots
1 to 2 hot red chilies, seeded and
     finely chopped*
2 tablespoons hoisin sauce
2 tablespoons sesame oil
4 cloves garlic, minced

1 tablespoon oyster sauce
1 tablespoon fresh lime juice
1 tablespoon sesame seed, toasted
2 teaspoons grated fresh
     gingerroot

1 lb. boneless skinless sharptail
     grouse meat, cut into strips
5 cups mixed baby greens
4 cups hot cooked Basmati rice

4 to 5 servings

In medium mixing bowl, combine all marinade ingredients. Add sharptail, stirring to coat. Cover with plastic wrap. Refrigerate overnight, stirring occasionally.

Using slotted spoon, remove sharptail from marinade. Place marinade in 1-quart saucepan and bring to a boil over medium heat. Remove from heat. Heat 12-inch nonstick skillet over high heat. Add sharptail. Cook for 4 to 6 minutes, or until meat is desired doneness, stirring frequently.

On large serving platter, spread greens evenly. Top with rice. Spoon sharp-tail over rice. Drizzle some of reserved marinade over top. Serve remaining marinade on the side.

For more heat, do not remove seeds from chilies.

Per Serving: Calories: 560 • Protein: 30 g. • Carbohydrate: 71 g. • Fat: 10 g.
• Cholesterol: 60 mg. • Sodium: 1966 mg.
Exchanges: 2¾ starch, 3¼ lean meat, ½ vegetable, 1 fruit

Cucumber-Yogurt Salad

This cooling salad is a perfect accompaniment to the hot and spicy sharptail. Blanching the cucumbers keeps them crisp.

2 medium cucumbers
4 cups water
½ cup plain yogurt
½ cup sour cream
2 tablespoons chopped walnuts,
     toasted
1 tablespoon shredded coconut,
     toasted
2 teaspoons finely chopped fresh
     parsley
½ teaspoon dried dill weed
¼ teaspoon salt

4 to 6 servings

Peel cucumbers. Cut cucumbers in half lengthwise, remove seeds with spoon, and slice. In 3-quart saucepan, bring water to a boil over high heat. Add cucumbers. Cook for 2 minutes, stirring occasionally. Quickly drain cucumbers and rinse with cold water until cool. Drain well and pat cucumbers dry with paper towels.

In medium mixing bowl, combine remaining ingredients. Add cucumbers. Toss to coat. Cover with plastic wrap. Chill at least 1 hour to allow flavors to blend.

Per Serving: Calories: 83 • Protein: 2 g.
• Carbohydrate: 5 g. • Fat: 6 g.
• Cholesterol: 10 mg. • Sodium: 118 mg.
Exchanges: ½ vegetable, 1¼ fat

Chutney-Ginger Sharptail ↑

1	whole acorn squash (about 1½ lbs.), sliced into 1-inch rings, seeds removed
1½	cups apple juice
1	medium red cooking apple, cored and chopped (1 cup)
½	cup fresh cranberries
1	small onion, chopped (½ cup)
1	tablespoon fresh thyme leaves
2	sticks cinnamon (2-inch lengths)
2	tablespoons olive oil
1	clove garlic, minced
1	teaspoon ground ginger
½	teaspoon ground cardamom
½	teaspoon salt
¼	teaspoon white pepper
1	whole dressed sharptail grouse (¾ to 1 lb.), skin removed, quartered
¼	cup prepared mango chutney
4	sprigs fresh thyme for garnish

2 servings

Heat oven to 350°F. Arrange squash rings in 13 × 9-inch baking dish. Set aside. In medium mixing bowl, combine juice, apple, cranberries, onion, thyme leaves and cinnamon. Spoon mixture evenly over squash. Set aside.

In 12-inch nonstick skillet, heat oil over medium heat. Add garlic, ginger, cardamom, salt and pepper. Cook for 30 seconds, stirring constantly. Add sharptail. Cook for 6 to 8 minutes, or until meat is browned, turning pieces occasionally.

Arrange sharptail over squash and apple mixture. Brush pieces evenly with chutney. Cook for 1 to 1¼ hours, or until squash is tender. To serve, arrange squash rings on serving plates. Top with fruit mixture, then sharptail pieces. Garnish with sprigs of fresh thyme. Serve with additional chutney, if desired.

Per Serving: Calories: 706 • Protein: 39 g. • Carbohydrate: 95 g. • Fat: 20 g.
• Cholesterol: 100 mg. • Sodium: 959 mg.
Exchanges: 1¾ starch, 4¾ very lean meat, 1 vegetable, 2¼ fruit, 4 fat

Herbed Sharptail Sauté ● VERY FAST

¼	cup all-purpose flour
2	teaspoons dried parsley flakes, crushed
½	teaspoon paprika
½	teaspoon dried rosemary leaves, crushed
¼	teaspoon salt
¼	teaspoon pepper
1	lb. boneless skinless sharptail grouse meat, cut into 1-inch pieces
2	tablespoons olive oil
2	tablespoons butter or margarine
2	cloves garlic, minced
4	cups hot cooked egg noodles

4 servings

In sealable plastic bag, combine flour, parsley, paprika, rosemary, salt and pepper. Add sharptail. Seal bag; shake to coat. Set aside.

In 12-inch nonstick skillet, heat oil and butter over medium heat. Add garlic. Cook for 1 minute, stirring constantly. Add sharptail. Cook for 5 to 7 minutes, or until meat is browned and desired doneness, stirring frequently. Spoon sharptail and pan drippings over noodles, tossing to coat.

Per Serving: Calories: 507 • Protein: 35 g.
• Carbohydrate: 47 g. • Fat: 19 g.
• Cholesterol: 143 mg. • Sodium: 248 mg.
Exchanges: 2¾ starch, 4 very lean meat, 3¾ fat

Moroccan Grilled Sharptail

RUB:

    2 tablespoons sliced green onion
    2 tablespoons snipped fresh cilantro
    2 tablespoons snipped fresh parsley
 1½ teaspoons paprika
 1½ teaspoons ground cumin
    1 clove garlic, minced
    1 teaspoon salt
  ¼ cup butter, softened

    2 whole dressed sharptail (¾ to 1 lb. each), skin removed, quartered

4 servings

In small bowl, combine all rub ingredients, except butter. Crush with back of spoon until blended. Stir in butter until well combined.

Rinse sharptail with cold water and pat dry with paper towels. Rub pieces all over with ¾ of rub mixture. Cover with plastic wrap. Refrigerate 1 hour.

Prepare grill for medium direct heat. Arrange sharptail pieces on cooking grid. Grill for 15 to 18 minutes, or until meat is desired doneness, turning pieces over once or twice and brushing occasionally with remaining rub mixture.

Per Serving: Calories: 312 • Protein: 36 g.
• Carbohydrate: 1 g. • Fat: 17 g.
• Cholesterol: 131 mg.
• Sodium: 727 mg.
Exchanges: 5¼ very lean meat, ¼ vegetable, 3 fat

Sharptail Soup with Caraway Dumplings ↓

    1 small onion, chopped (½ cup)
    3 slices bacon, chopped
  12 oz. boneless skinless sharptail grouse meat, cut into ¾-inch cubes
    3 cans (14½ oz. each) ready-to-serve chicken broth
    1 bottle (12 oz.) lager-style beer
    2 cups baby carrots
    2 cups chopped red potatoes
  ½ cup chopped white cabbage

  ½ teaspoon garlic powder
  ½ teaspoon salt
  ½ teaspoon pepper
    1 cup 2% milk
  ½ cup all-purpose flour

DUMPLINGS:
    2 cups buttermilk baking mix
  ⅔ cup 2% milk
    1 teaspoon caraway seed

6 to 8 servings

In 6-quart Dutch oven or stockpot, combine onion and bacon. Cook over medium-high heat for 2 to 3 minutes, or until onion is tender-crisp. Add sharptail. Cook for 3 to 4 minutes, or until meat is browned, stirring occasionally.

Add broth, beer, carrots, potatoes, cabbage, garlic powder, salt and pepper. Bring to a boil. Cover. Reduce heat to medium-low. Simmer for 10 to 15 minutes, or until vegetables are tender.

In 2-cup measure, combine 1 cup milk and the flour. Stir milk mixture into soup. Cook for 2 to 3 minutes, or until soup is thickened, stirring occasionally.

In medium mixing bowl, combine dumpling ingredients. Stir until soft dough forms. Drop dumplings by tablespoonfuls into soup. Cover. Cook for 10 to 12 minutes, or until dumplings are no longer doughy.

Per Serving: Calories: 372 • Protein: 18 g. • Carbohydrate: 40 g. • Fat: 13 g.
• Cholesterol: 38 mg. • Sodium: 1276 mg.
Exchanges: 2 starch, 1½ very lean meat, ½ vegetable, ¼ low-fat milk, 2½ fat

Hungarian Partridge with Juniper

2 whole dressed Hungarian partridges (¾ to 1 lb. each), skin removed, halved
Salt and pepper to taste
2 tablespoons butter or margarine
2 medium carrots, sliced (1 cup)
2 stalks celery, sliced (1 cup)
1 medium onion, chopped (1 cup)
2 cups water or chicken broth
¼ cup brandy
10 dried juniper berries, crushed
1 bay leaf
¼ teaspoon dried thyme leaves
1 sprig fresh parsley
8 oz. fresh mushrooms, quartered

4 servings

Heat oven to 400°F. Sprinkle partridge halves with salt and pepper to taste. In 12-inch nonstick skillet, melt butter over medium heat. Add partridges and cook for 4 to 6 minutes, or until browned, turning occasionally. Set aside.

In 13 × 9-inch baking dish, evenly spread carrots, celery and onion. Add water, brandy, juniper berries, bay leaf, thyme and parsley. Arrange partridge halves over vegetables. Arrange mushrooms around partridges. Cover with foil. Bake for 45 to 55 minutes, or until vegetables and meat are tender. Remove and discard bay leaf.

Per Serving: Calories: 300 • Protein: 38 g.
• Carbohydrate: 10 g. • Fat: 12 g.
• Cholesterol: 116 mg. • Sodium: 154 mg.
Exchanges: 5 very lean meat, 2 vegetable, 2¼ fat

Hungarian Partridge Hunter's Style VERY FAST

2 whole dressed Hungarian partridges (¾ to 1 lb. each), skin removed, halved
2 tablespoons butter or margarine
1 small head white cabbage, shredded (5 cups)
4 slices bacon, halved

2 spicy link sausages* (3 oz. each), sliced
2 medium carrots, sliced (1 cup)
1 medium onion, sliced
4 juniper berries, crushed
1 can (14½ oz.) ready-to-serve chicken broth
1 teaspoon grated lemon peel

4 servings

Heat oven to 350°F. Rinse birds with cold water and pat dry with paper towels. In 12-inch nonstick skillet, melt butter over medium-high heat. Add partridge halves. Cook for 5 to 7 minutes, or until browned, turning partridges occasionally.

In bottom of 13 × 9-inch baking dish, spread cabbage evenly. Arrange partridge halves over cabbage. Place 1 slice bacon over each partridge half. Arrange sausages, carrots, onion and juniper berries around partridges. Pour broth into bottom of dish. Top evenly with peel. Cover with foil. Bake for 45 to 55 minutes, or until meat and vegetables are tender.

*Andouille sausage, a spicy Cajun-style sausage, is recommended, but any spicy sausage will work.

Per Serving: Calories: 619 • Protein: 46 g. • Carbohydrate: 12 g. • Fat: 43 g.
• Cholesterol: 160 mg. • Sodium: 1018 mg.
Exchanges: 5¾ lean meat, 2¼ vegetable, 5 fat

Hungarian Partridge Scaloppini

2 whole boneless skinless Hungarian partridge
   breasts (6 oz. each), split in half, pounded
   to ¼-inch thickness
   Salt and pepper to taste
2 tablespoons olive oil
2 tablespoons butter or margarine, divided
2 tablespoons fresh lemon juice
2 teaspoons capers, drained
2 tablespoons snipped fresh parsley
   Lemon slices for garnish

4 servings

Sprinkle partridge breasts with salt and pepper to taste. In 12-inch nonstick skillet, heat oil and 1 tablespoon butter over medium-high heat. Add breasts. Cook for 5 to 7 minutes, or until meat is browned, turning breasts over once. Set breasts aside and keep warm.

Reduce heat to medium-low. Add juice and capers to skillet. Stir in remaining 1 tablespoon butter until melted. Stir in parsley. Spoon sauce over partridge breasts. Garnish with lemon slices.

Per Serving: Calories: 227 • Protein: 20 g. • Carbohydrate: 1 g. • Fat: 16 g. • Cholesterol: 72 mg. • Sodium: 154 mg. Exchanges: 3 very lean meat, 3 fat

Peppered Partridge Paprikash

- 3 tablespoons olive oil
- 1 medium onion, chopped (1 cup)
- 1½ cups dry white wine
- 1 tablespoon plus 1½ teaspoons sweet Hungarian paprika
- ½ teaspoon salt
- ¼ teaspoon white pepper
- 1 lb. boneless skinless Hungarian partridge meat, cut into 1-inch cubes
- 1 green pepper, seeded and sliced
- 1 red pepper, seeded and sliced
- 1 yellow pepper, seeded and sliced
- 1 cup sour cream
- 1 tablespoon all-purpose flour
- 4 cups hot cooked wide egg noodles
- ¼ cup snipped fresh parsley

4 servings

In 6-quart Dutch oven or stockpot, heat oil over medium heat. Add onion. Cook for 6 to 8 minutes, or until golden, stirring occasionally. Stir in wine, paprika, salt and pepper. Bring to a simmer. Add partridge. Cover. Simmer for 45 to 50 minutes, or until meat is tender, stirring occasionally. Stir in green, red and yellow peppers during last 10 minutes of cooking.

In small mixing bowl, combine sour cream and flour. Gradually whisk mixture into pot. Cook for 4 to 6 minutes, or until thickened and heated through. Serve paprikash over noodles. Sprinkle with parsley.

Per Serving: Calories: 626 • Protein: 38 g.
• Carbohydrate: 53 g. • Fat: 29 g.
• Cholesterol: 153 mg. • Sodium: 366 mg.
Exchanges: 3 starch, 4 very lean meat,
1 vegetable, 5½ fat

Artichoke & Parmesan Stuffed Partridge Rolls

1 can (14 oz.) artichoke hearts in water, drained
1 cup shredded fresh Parmesan cheese
½ cup sliced green onions
¼ cup mayonnaise
2 cloves garlic, minced
¼ teaspoon white pepper
8 whole boneless skinless Hungarian partridge breasts (6 oz. each), split in half
16 slices prosciutto ham (2 × 3-inch slices)
¼ cup butter, melted
2 cups warm prepared marinara sauce

8 servings

Heat oven to 350°F. In blender or food processor, combine artichoke hearts, Parmesan cheese, onions, mayonnaise, garlic and pepper. Process until nearly smooth. Set aside. Spray 13 × 9-inch baking dish with nonstick vegetable cooking spray. Set aside.

Place partridge breasts between two sheets of wax paper. Pound breasts to ¼-inch thickness. Place 1 slice prosciutto on top of each breast half. Spread 1 heaping tablespoon artichoke mixture over each slice prosciutto. Roll breast halves jelly-roll-style; secure with wooden picks.

Arrange partridge rolls in prepared dish. Drizzle rolls with butter. Cover with foil. Bake for 20 minutes. Remove foil. Bake for 5 to 10 minutes longer, or until meat is no longer pink. Spoon ¼ cup marinara sauce on each serving plate. Top with 2 partridge rolls.

Per Serving: Calories: 472 • Protein: 53 g.
• Carbohydrate: 10 g. • Fat: 25 g.
• Cholesterol: 139 mg. • Sodium: 1037 mg.
Exchanges: 7 very lean meat,
1¼ vegetable, 5 fat

Horseradish Prairie Chicken

2 whole dressed prairie chickens (1 to 1¾ lbs. each), skin on
1 medium red cooking apple, sliced (1 cup)
1 stalk celery, sliced (½ cup)
3 tablespoons butter
1 medium onion, halved and sliced
2 slices bacon, halved
1 cup ready-to-serve chicken broth
¼ cup brandy
  Freshly ground pepper to taste
1 cup sour cream
2 tablespoons grated fresh horseradish

4 to 6 servings

Heat oven to 350°F. Stuff cavities of prairie chickens evenly with apple and celery. In 12-inch skillet, melt butter over medium heat. Add onion. Cook for 2 minutes, stirring occasionally. Add prairie chickens. Cook for 5 to 7 minutes, or until browned, turning chickens occasionally.

Arrange chickens breast-side-up in 13 × 9-inch roasting pan. Arrange onion around chickens. Place bacon strips evenly across chickens. Pour broth and brandy into pan. Sprinkle chickens evenly with pepper. Cover. Roast for 1 hour. Uncover. Increase heat to 375°F. Roast for 15 to 20 minutes, or until chickens are browned and meat is tender, basting occasionally.

Arrange chickens on serving platter. Set aside and keep warm. Transfer pan drippings to 1-quart saucepan. Whisk sour cream and horseradish into pan drippings. Cook over medium heat for 2 to 3 minutes, or until heated through, stirring constantly. Serve sauce with chickens.

Per Serving: Calories: 530 • Protein: 43 g. • Carbohydrate: 8 g. • Fat: 35 g.
• Cholesterol: 165 mg. • Sodium: 379 mg.
Exchanges: 5¾ lean meat, 1 vegetable, ¼ fruit, 3½ fat

Prairie Chicken & Roasted Peppers

VERY FAST

½ teaspoon ground cumin
½ teaspoon pepper
½ teaspoon dried oregano leaves
½ teaspoon garlic powder
 2 whole dressed prairie chickens (1 to 1¾ lbs. each), skin removed, cut into pieces
 3 tablespoons olive oil
 1 medium onion, thinly sliced
 1 jar (12 oz.) roasted red pepper strips, drained
 2 Anaheim chilies, roasted*, peeled and cut into ½-inch strips

4 to 6 servings

In small mixing bowl, combine cumin, pepper, oregano and garlic powder. Rub mixture evenly over prairie chicken pieces.

In 12-inch skillet, heat oil over medium-high heat. Add prairie chicken pieces. Cook for 4 to 6 minutes, or until browned, turning pieces occasionally. Reduce heat to medium-low. Add onion, red pepper and chilies. Cover. Cook for 15 to 18 minutes, or until meat is no longer pink and onion is tender.

*To roast chilies, place them under broiler with surface 2 to 4 inches from heat. Broil until skin blackens and blisters, turning chilies frequently. Place chilies in plastic or paper bag for 10 minutes. Peel chilies and proceed as directed.

Per Serving:
Calories: 307
• Protein: 38 g.
• Carbohydrate: 8 g.
• Fat: 13 g.
• Cholesterol: 104 mg.
• Sodium: 180 mg.
Exchanges: 5 very lean meat, 1½ vegetable, 2½ fat

Roasted Prairie Chicken with Potatoes ↓

 1 whole dressed prairie chicken (1 to 1¾ lbs.), skin on
¼ cup chopped onion
 1 lb. Yukon Gold or Yellow Finn potatoes, cut into 1½-inch pieces
 1 teaspoon dried thyme leaves
   Freshly ground pepper to taste
 1 cup hot water
 2 teaspoons chicken bouillon granules
 2 cloves garlic, minced

2 to 3 servings

Heat oven to 350°F. Stuff cavity of prairie chicken with onion. Place chicken in 13 × 9-inch roasting pan. Arrange potatoes around chicken. Sprinkle evenly with thyme and pepper. In 1-cup measure, combine water, bouillon and garlic. Pour mixture into pan. Cover.

Roast for 45 minutes. Uncover. Roast for 30 to 40 minutes longer, or until chicken and potatoes are tender and browned, basting occasionally.

Per Serving: Calories: 464 • Protein: 44 g. • Carbohydrate: 30 g.
• Fat: 17 g. • Cholesterol: 128 mg. • Sodium: 779 mg.
Exchanges: 1¾ starch, 5¾ lean meat, ¼ vegetable

Prairie Chicken & Vegetable Soup LOW-FAT ↓

2 teaspoons vegetable oil
1 lb. boneless skinless prairie chicken meat, cut into ¾-inch pieces
1 small onion, chopped (½ cup)
2 cloves garlic, minced
2 stalks celery, sliced (1 cup)
2 medium carrots, sliced (1 cup)
6 cups water
1 can (14½ oz.) stewed tomatoes
1 tablespoon beef bouillon granules
½ teaspoon dried basil leaves
½ teaspoon salt
½ teaspoon freshly ground pepper
1 pkg. (9 oz.) frozen mixed vegetables

6 servings

In 4-quart saucepan, heat oil over medium heat. Add prairie chicken, onion and garlic. Cook for 4 to 6 minutes, or until meat is no longer pink, stirring occasionally. Add celery and carrots. Cook for 3 to 4 minutes, or until celery brightens in color, stirring occasionally.

Stir in remaining ingredients, except frozen vegetables. Bring to a boil over high heat. Cover. Reduce heat to medium-low. Simmer for 10 minutes, stirring occasionally. Stir in frozen vegetables. Re-cover. Cook for 10 to 15 minutes, or until vegetables are tender, stirring occasionally.

TIP: If a thinner soup is desired, add more water.

Per Serving: Calories: 180 • Protein: 21 g. • Carbohydrate: 15 g. • Fat: 5 g. • Cholesterol: 50 mg. • Sodium: 849 mg.
Exchanges: ¼ starch, 2½ very lean meat, 2 vegetable, ¾ fat

Five-spice Prairie Chicken LOW-FAT

2 whole dressed prairie chickens (1 to 1¾ lbs. each), skin removed, quartered
1 tablespoon sesame oil
¾ teaspoon five-spice powder*
¼ teaspoon garlic powder
¼ teaspoon salt

4 to 6 servings

Heat oven to 400°F. Arrange prairie chicken pieces in 13 × 9-inch baking pan. Brush evenly with oil. Sprinkle evenly with five-spice powder, garlic powder and salt. Cover with foil.

Bake for 20 minutes. Remove foil. Bake for 35 to 45 minutes longer, or until meat is browned and tender.

Five-spice powder is a prepared blend of five spices used in Oriental cooking. It can be found in the Oriental section of your supermarket.

Per Serving: Calories: 232 • Protein: 37 g. • Carbohydrate: <1 g. • Fat: 8 g. • Cholesterol: 104 mg. • Sodium: 149 mg. Exchanges: 5¼ very lean meat, 1½ fat

Sage Grouse with Figs & Apricots →

MARINADE:

- ¾ cup dried apricots
- ½ cup coarsely chopped dried figs
- ⅓ cup red wine vinegar
- ⅓ cup olive oil
- 1 tablespoon dried thyme leaves
- 3 cloves garlic, minced
- 1½ teaspoons ground cumin
- 1 teaspoon coarsely ground pepper
- ½ teaspoon ground ginger
- ½ teaspoon salt

- 1 whole dressed sage grouse (2 to 2½ lbs.), skin removed, cut into pieces
- 2 tablespoons packed brown sugar
- ¼ cup tawny port
- ½ cup pecan halves
- 2 teaspoons grated lemon peel

4 servings

In sealable plastic bag, combine marinade ingredients. Add grouse pieces. Seal bag; turn to coat pieces. Refrigerate several hours or overnight, turning bag occasionally.

Heat oven to 350°F. Place grouse pieces and marinade in 9-inch square baking dish. Sprinkle evenly with sugar. Pour port into dish. Cover with foil.

Bake for 20 minutes. Remove foil. Bake for 35 to 45 minutes longer, or until meat is tender, basting occasionally. Serve grouse on platter surrounded with fruit from marinade. Drizzle with pan drippings. Sprinkle with pecans and peel.

Per Serving: Calories: 675 • Protein: 49 g.
• Carbohydrate: 45 g. • Fat: 35 g.
• Cholesterol: 128 mg. • Sodium: 357 mg.
Exchanges: 7 very lean meat, 2 fruit, 6 fat

Danish-pickled Spruce Grouse 🔵 LOW-FAT

Preparing grouse in this unusual way makes the meat flaky and sweet. Serve it on crackers with cream cheese and chives.

- 1 lb. boneless skinless spruce grouse meat, cut into very large pieces
- 4 cups water
- 1 cup dry red wine
- 1 tablespoon salt

- 3 bay leaves
- 10 whole juniper berries
- 8 whole peppercorns
- 1 clove garlic, crushed
- 1 teaspoon whole allspice

10 to 12 appetizer servings

In 4-quart saucepan, combine all ingredients. Bring to a boil over high heat. Cover. Reduce heat to medium-low. Simmer for 2 to 2½ hours, or until meat is very tender.

Transfer meat and liquid to large, nonmetallic bowl. Cool completely. Cover with plastic wrap. Refrigerate 2 to 3 days, stirring occasionally. Drain and discard liquid from meat. Using fork, flake meat into small pieces. Refrigerate in airtight container for up to 1 week.

Per Serving: Calories: 52 • Protein: 9 g. • Carbohydrate: <1 g. • Fat: 1 g.
• Cholesterol: 25 mg. • Sodium: 289 mg.
Exchanges: 1¼ very lean meat, ¼ fat

Sage Grouse Soup with Dumplings ⏱FAST

¼ cup butter or margarine
6 medium carrots, cut into
    ½-inch chunks
5 small onions, each cut into
    6 wedges
1 stalk celery, sliced
6 tablespoons all-purpose flour
12 cups ready-to-serve chicken
    broth
2 lbs. boneless skinless sage
    grouse meat, cut into 1-inch
    pieces
1 teaspoon dried thyme leaves
1 teaspoon dried marjoram leaves
¼ teaspoon pepper
1 can (10 oz.) refrigerated biscuit
    dough
½ cup half-and-half
    Snipped fresh parsley (optional)

8 to 10 servings

In 6-quart Dutch oven or stockpot, melt butter over medium heat. Add carrots, onions and celery. Cook for 3 to 4 minutes, or until onions begin to soften, stirring occasionally. Stir in flour. Cook for 1 minute, stirring constantly.

Gradually blend in broth. Stir in grouse, thyme, marjoram and pepper. Bring to a boil over high heat. Reduce heat to medium-low. Simmer for 5 to 7 minutes, or until soup is thickened, stirring frequently.

Separate biscuit dough and cut individual biscuits in half. Drop dough pieces on top of simmering soup. Simmer, uncovered, for 10 minutes. Cover. Simmer for 10 minutes longer, or until biscuits are no longer doughy.

Remove from heat. Push dumplings to side of pan; slowly stir in half-and-half. Sprinkle individual servings with parsley.

Per Serving: Calories: 351 • Protein: 28 g.
• Carbohydrate: 26 g. • Fat: 16 g.
• Cholesterol: 77 mg. • Sodium: 1606 mg.
Exchanges: 1 starch, 3 very lean meat,
2 vegetable, 3 fat

Red-wine Marinated Spruce Grouse (LOW-FAT)

MARINADE:

1/3 cup soy sauce
1/3 cup dry red wine
3 tablespoons white wine vinegar
3 tablespoons olive oil
2 tablespoons Worcestershire sauce
2 to 3 cloves garlic, minced
2 teaspoons dried rosemary leaves
    Coarsely ground pepper to taste
2 whole dressed spruce grouse
    (3/4 to 1 lb. each), skin
    removed, halved

3 to 4 servings

In sealable plastic bag, combine marinade ingredients. Add grouse. Seal bag; turn to coat. Refrigerate several hours or overnight, turning bag occasionally.

Prepare grill for medium direct heat. Spray cooking grid with nonstick vegetable cooking spray. Drain and discard marinade from grouse. Arrange grouse pieces on cooking grid. Grill for 15 to 18 minutes, or until meat is no longer pink, turning grouse occasionally.

Per Serving: Calories: 234 • Protein: 36 g.
• Carbohydrate: 1 g. • Fat: 8 g.
• Cholesterol: 100 mg. • Sodium: 406 mg.
Exchanges: 5 very lean meat, 1½ fat

Sage Grouse with Artichokes & Mushrooms ↓

2 whole boneless skinless sage
    grouse breasts (8 to 10 oz.
    each), split in half
1/4 teaspoon salt
6 tablespoons butter or
    margarine, divided
8 oz. fresh mushrooms, sliced
    (3 cups)
1 jar (7 oz.) artichoke hearts in
    marinade, drained and halved
1/2 teaspoon dried tarragon
    leaves
2 tablespoons all-purpose flour
3/4 cup ready-to-serve chicken
    broth
1/4 cup dry sherry
1 tablespoon snipped fresh
    parsley

4 servings

Heat oven to 375°F. Sprinkle grouse breasts evenly with salt. In 12-inch skillet, melt 2 tablespoons butter over medium-high heat. Add grouse breasts. Cook for 4 to 6 minutes, or until meat is browned, turning breasts over once. Arrange breasts in 12 × 8-inch baking dish. Set aside.

Add 2 tablespoons butter to drippings in skillet. Melt over medium heat. Add mushrooms. Cook for 3 to 4 minutes, or until mushrooms are tender, stirring occasionally. Using slotted spoon, spoon mushrooms over grouse breasts. Top with artichoke hearts and tarragon. Set aside.

Add remaining 2 tablespoons butter to drippings in skillet. Melt over medium heat. Whisk flour into drippings. Cook for 1 minute, stirring constantly. Gradually blend in broth. Cook for 3 to 4 minutes, or until sauce is thickened and bubbly, stirring constantly. Remove from heat. Stir in sherry.

Pour sauce over grouse. Bake for 30 to 45 minutes, or until meat is no longer pink. Sprinkle with parsley. Serve over rice pilaf, if desired.

Per Serving: Calories: 423 • Protein: 34 g. • Carbohydrate: 10 g.
• Fat: 26 g. • Cholesterol: 121 mg. • Sodium: 800 mg.
Exchanges: 4½ very lean meat,
1¼ vegetable, 5 fat

Light–Small Birds

Broiled Quail

This very simple technique can be used to quickly cook quail while bringing out its delicate flavor.

  8 whole dressed quail (4 to 6 oz. each), skin on
½ cup butter or margarine, melted
    Salt and pepper to taste

8 servings

Split each quail down the back, and flatten.

Spray rack in broiler pan with nonstick vegetable cooking spray. Set aside. Brush both sides of quail lightly with butter. Sprinkle salt and pepper evenly over quail. Arrange quail breast-side-up on rack in broiler pan.

Place quail under broiler with surface of meat 4 to 5 inches from heat. Broil for 5 to 6 minutes, or until lightly browned. Brush quail with some of remaining butter. Turn quail over. Broil for 5 to 6 minutes, or until lightly browned. Brush and turn quail again. Broil for 3 to 5 minutes longer, or until meat is tender and juices run clear.

Per Serving: Calories: 293 • Protein: 25 g. • Carbohydrate: 0 g.
• Fat: 21 g. • Cholesterol: 111 mg. • Sodium: 125 mg.
Exchanges: 3½ lean meat, 2 fat

Cranberry-Apple Chutney   LOW-FAT

This flavorful chutney is a great accompaniment for wild game birds and meats. It makes a large batch, so refrigerate or freeze the extra for future use.

  1 pkg. (16 oz.) fresh or frozen cranberries
  1 cup water
¾ cup sugar
¾ cup packed brown sugar
½ cup golden raisins
  2 teaspoons ground cinnamon
1½ teaspoons ground ginger
½ teaspoon ground nutmeg
¼ teaspoon ground cloves
  2 medium cooking apples, peeled, cored and chopped (2½ cups)
  1 medium onion, chopped (1 cup)

16 servings (4 cups)

In 2-quart saucepan, combine cranberries, water, sugars, raisins, cinnamon, ginger, nutmeg and cloves. Cook over medium heat for 10 to 15 minutes, or until cranberries burst, stirring occasionally.

Stir in apples and onion. Reduce heat to low. Simmer for 12 to 15 minutes, or until mixture is thickened and apples are tender-crisp, stirring occasionally. Store unused chutney in airtight container in refrigerator for up to 2 weeks.

TIP: Make the chutney a day or two in advance and reheat over low heat just before serving.

Per Serving: Calories: 118 • Protein: <1 g. • Carbohydrate: 30 g.
• Fat: <1 g. • Cholesterol: 0 mg. • Sodium: 5 mg.
Exchanges: ¾ fruit

Roast Quail with Sherry Crumbs & Cream Sauce

1½ cups 2% milk
6 tablespoons butter or margarine, divided
⅓ cup finely chopped onion
2 cloves garlic, minced
6 whole cloves
1 bay leaf
1 sprig fresh thyme
4 whole dressed quail (4 to 6 oz. each), skin on
Salt and pepper to taste
4 slices bacon
2 cups very coarse fresh bread crumbs
⅓ cup dry sherry
2 tablespoons snipped fresh parsley
1 tablespoon all-purpose flour

4 servings

In 1-quart saucepan, combine milk, 3 tablespoons butter, the onion, garlic, cloves, bay leaf and thyme. Bring to a boil over medium-high heat, stirring frequently. Reduce heat to low. Simmer for 10 minutes. Remove from heat. Set sauce aside.

Heat oven to 425°F. Sprinkle quail evenly with salt and pepper. Wrap bacon crosswise across top of each quail. Tuck ends of bacon under back of quail. Place quail breast-side-up in 10 × 6-inch baking pan. Cover with foil. Bake for 20 to 25 minutes, or until meat is tender and juices run clear. Remove foil. Baste quail with pan drippings. Bake for 10 to 15 minutes longer, or until lightly browned. Remove quail from oven and keep warm.

Meanwhile, in 10-inch skillet, melt remaining 3 tablespoons butter over medium heat. Add crumbs, stirring to coat. Cook crumbs for 4 to 6 minutes, or until golden brown, stirring frequently. Reduce heat to low. Stir in sherry. Cook for 1 to 2 minutes, or until liquid is boiled away, stirring frequently. Stir in parsley and salt and pepper to taste. Remove from heat. Set aside and keep warm.

Strain sauce through fine-mesh sieve into 1-quart saucepan. Whisk in flour. Cook over medium-high heat for 3 to 5 minutes, or until mixture is thickened and bubbly, stirring constantly. Season with salt and pepper to taste.

To serve, place quail on individual serving plates. Spoon crumbs evenly over quail and spoon some sauce over and around quail. Serve quail with any additional sauce.

Per Serving: Calories: 579 • Protein: 32 g. • Carbohydrate: 20 g. • Fat: 38 g.
• Cholesterol: 156 mg. • Sodium: 504 mg.
Exchanges: 1 starch, 3¾ lean meat, ½ low-fat milk, 5 fat

Polenta Quail

POLENTA:

- 4 cups ready-to-serve chicken broth
- 1 cup yellow cornmeal
- 1 tablespoon olive oil
- 1 tablespoon snipped fresh parsley
- 2 teaspoons fresh thyme leaves
  Salt to taste (optional)

- 4 whole dressed quail (4 to 6 oz. each), skin on
- 1 tablespoon olive oil
- ½ teaspoon coarse salt
- ¼ cup finely chopped onion
- 4 sprigs fresh thyme leaves
- 8 strips bacon

SAUCE:

- 1 tablespoon olive oil
- 1 small onion, chopped (½ cup)
- 1 clove garlic, minced
- 1 large tomato, seeded and chopped (1¼ cups)
- ½ cup ready-to-serve chicken broth
- ¼ cup dry red wine
  Salt and pepper to taste

4 servings

Spray 8-inch square baking pan with nonstick vegetable cooking spray. Set aside. To make polenta, bring 4 cups broth to a simmer over medium heat. Add cornmeal in slow, steady stream, stirring constantly with wooden spoon. Stir in 1 tablespoon oil, the parsley, thyme and salt. Cook for 15 to 20 minutes, or until polenta pulls away from sides of pan, stirring constantly. Spoon polenta into prepared pan, spreading evenly. Set aside.

Heat oven to 425°F. Brush cavity of each quail evenly with 1 tablespoon oil. Sprinkle cavities evenly with coarse salt, then place 1 tablespoon finely chopped onion and 1 sprig thyme in each. Secure legs of quail with kitchen string. Wrap each quail with 2 strips bacon. Place quail in shallow roasting pan. Roast quail for 25 to 30 minutes, or until meat is tender and juices run clear.

Meanwhile, in 12-inch nonstick skillet, heat 1 tablespoon oil over medium heat. Add ½ cup onion and the garlic. Cook for 4 to 6 minutes, or until onion is golden. Stir in tomato, ½ cup broth and the wine. Simmer for 10 to 12 minutes, or until liquid is reduced, stirring occasionally. Season sauce to taste with salt and pepper. Set aside and keep warm.

Warm polenta by placing it in hot oven with quail for a few minutes. Cut polenta into 4 equal pieces. On individual serving plates, top 1 piece of polenta with 1 quail. Spoon sauce over or around quail.

Per Serving: Calories: 605 • Protein: 35 g. • Carbohydrate: 33 g. • Fat: 35 g.
• Cholesterol: 107 mg. • Sodium: 1586 mg.
Exchanges: 1¾ starch, 4 lean meat, 1 vegetable, 4½ fat

Portobello Quail

4 large portobello mushrooms
5 tablespoons olive oil, divided
1 medium onion, chopped
    (1 cup)
1 tablespoon fresh thyme leaves
4 whole dressed quail (4 to 6 oz.
    each), skin on
    Salt and pepper to taste
¼ cup balsamic vinegar

4 servings

Per Serving: Calories: 445 • Protein: 28 g.
• Carbohydrate: 11 g. • Fat: 33 g.
• Cholesterol: 96 mg. • Sodium: 75 mg.
Exchanges: ½ starch, 3½ lean meat,
1 vegetable, 4¼ fat

Remove stems from mushrooms; chop stems. Set aside. In 12-inch non-stick skillet, heat 2 tablespoons oil over medium heat. Add mushroom caps. Cook for 4 to 5 minutes, or until mushrooms are golden, turning caps once. Remove with slotted spoon. Set aside.

Add 1 tablespoon oil to skillet. Reduce heat to medium-low. Add onion, chopped mushroom stems and thyme. Cook for 15 to 18 minutes, or until onion is tender and golden, stirring occasionally.

Meanwhile, in 10-inch nonstick skillet, heat remaining 2 tablespoons oil over medium heat. Sprinkle surfaces and cavities of quail with salt and pepper. Cook quail in skillet for 18 to 20 minutes, or until browned on all sides, turning quail occasionally.

When onion is done, return caps to first skillet, top-side-down. Place 1 quail on each mushroom cap. Increase heat to medium. Pour vinegar into second skillet, stirring to loosen browned bits from bottom. Pour mixture around quail in first skillet. Simmer for 2 to 3 minutes, or until sauce is slightly reduced. Serve immediately.

Cherry-sauced Quail

4 whole dressed quail (4 to 6 oz. each), skin on
  Salt and pepper to taste
3 tablespoons butter or margarine

SAUCE:

1/3 cup dried sweetened cherries, halved
1/3 cup port wine
3 tablespoons cherry preserves
1/2 teaspoon grated lemon peel

4 servings

Heat oven to 400°F. Sprinkle surfaces and cavities of quail with salt and pepper. In 12-inch nonstick skillet, melt butter over medium-high heat. Add quail. Cook quail for 5 to 6 minutes, or until browned on all sides, turning quail frequently.

Arrange quail breast-side-up in 8-inch square baking dish. Cover with foil. Bake for 20 to 25 minutes, or until meat is tender and juices run clear.

Meanwhile, in 1-quart saucepan, combine sauce ingredients. Bring to a boil over medium heat. Boil for 1 minute, stirring frequently. Serve sauce with quail.

Per Serving: Calories: 413 • Protein: 25 g. • Carbohydrate: 20 g.
• Fat: 24 g. • Cholesterol: 119 mg. • Sodium: 163 mg.
Exchanges: 3 1/2 lean meat, 1/2 fruit, 2 1/2 fat

Grape Leaf Wrapped Quail ↑

4 whole dressed quail (4 to 6 oz. each), skin on
2 tablespoons chopped Kalamata olives
1 teaspoon dried oregano leaves
8 grape leaves in brine*, drained
2 tablespoons fresh lemon juice
2 tablespoons olive oil

4 servings

Heat oven to 425°F. Stuff quail evenly with chopped olives. Sprinkle surfaces of quail evenly with oregano, then wrap 2 grape leaves around each. Place wrapped quail in shallow roasting dish. In small bowl, combine juice and oil. Brush quail packets lightly with lemon mixture.

Bake quail for 25 to 30 minutes, or until meat is tender and juices run clear, brushing quail packets once or twice with remaining lemon mixture. Cut grape leaves open before serving quail.

*Grape leaves in brine are available in specialty markets or with the Greek olives in some super-markets. Fresh grape leaves may be substituted for brined leaves, but they should be soaked in water for at least 30 minutes before using.

Per Serving: Calories: 328 • Protein: 25 g. • Carbohydrate: 1 g.
• Fat: 23 g. • Cholesterol: 96 mg. • Sodium: 543 mg.
Exchanges: 3 1/2 lean meat, 1/4 vegetable, 2 1/2 fat

63

Grilled Quail & Sweet Potatoes

1 jalapeño pepper, seeded and finely chopped
2 tablespoons lime juice
1 teaspoon dried thyme leaves
1 clove garlic, minced
¼ teaspoon onion powder
4 whole dressed quail (4 to 6 oz. each), skin on
4 medium sweet potatoes (6 to 8 oz. each),
   unpeeled, halved lengthwise
¼ cup margarine or butter, melted

4 servings

In small mixing bowl, combine jalapeño, juice, thyme, garlic and onion powder. Rub mixture evenly over surfaces and in cavities of quail. Cover with plastic wrap. Chill 30 minutes.

Prepare grill for medium direct heat. Spray cooking grid with nonstick vegetable cooking spray. Brush quail and potatoes lightly with margarine. Place quail and potatoes on prepared grid. Grill, covered, for 20 to 25 minutes, or until meat and potatoes are tender, turning frequently and basting once or twice with remaining margarine.

TIP: Remove potatoes from grill as they become done. Return them to grill for 3 to 4 minutes to reheat when quail is done.

Per Serving: Calories: 558 • Protein: 28 g. • Carbohydrate: 50 g. • Fat: 27 g. • Cholesterol: 96 mg. • Sodium: 228 mg.
Exchanges: 3¼ starch, 3½ lean meat, 3¼ fat

Smoke-cooked Herbed Quail

MARINADE:

¼ cup white wine vinegar
2 teaspoons rubbed sage leaves
2 teaspoons Worcestershire sauce
1 clove garlic, minced
½ teaspoon dried oregano leaves
½ teaspoon sugar
½ teaspoon salt
¼ teaspoon dried thyme leaves
   Dash ground nutmeg
1 cup vegetable oil

4 whole dressed quail (4 to 6 oz.
   each), skin on
   Alder or hickory wood chips
4 slices bacon (optional)

4 servings

In food processor or blender, combine all marinade ingredients, except oil. Process until blended. With processor running, gradually add oil in slow drizzle until well blended. In shallow dish or sealable plastic bag, combine quail and marinade, turning to coat quail. Refrigerate several hours or overnight, turning quail occasionally.

Soak wood chips in warm water for 30 minutes; drain. Prepare grill for medium direct heat. Spray cooking grid with nonstick vegetable cooking spray. Drain and discard marinade from quail. Wrap each quail with 1 slice bacon.

Sprinkle a handful of wood chips over charcoal in grill. Cover grill until chips begin to smoke. Arrange quail on cooking grid. Grill, covered, for 10 to 15 minutes, or until meat is tender and juices run clear, turning quail occasionally.

Per Serving: Calories: 368 • Protein: 25 g.
• Carbohydrate: 1 g. • Fat: 29 g.
• Cholesterol: 96 mg. • Sodium: 216 mg.
Exchanges: 3½ lean meat, 3½ fat

Quail en Papillote ↓

4 whole dressed quail (4 to 6 oz.
   each), split in half, skin
   removed
   Salt and pepper to taste
1 small leek (white part only),
   cut into 2 × ¼-inch strips
1 medium carrot, cut into 2 ×
   ¼-inch strips

4 oz. snow pea pods, cut
   diagonally into ½-inch
   pieces
3½ oz. fresh enoki mushrooms
4 tablespoons butter or
   margarine

4 servings

Heat oven to 400°F. Cut four 12-inch squares of kitchen parchment paper. Sprinkle both sides of quail halves with salt and pepper. Place 2 quail halves in center of each square of parchment paper. Arrange leek, carrot, pea pods and mushrooms evenly around quail. Top each quail with 1 tablespoon butter.

Fold opposite sides of paper together in locked folds. Fold up edges in locked folds, rolling slightly to secure. Place packets on baking sheet, seam-side-up. Bake for 30 to 35 minutes, or until meat is tender and juices run clear. To serve, place packets seam-side-down on serving plates, cut "X" across packet and fold back edges.

Per Serving: Calories: 285 • Protein: 25 g. • Carbohydrate: 8 g. • Fat: 17 g.
• Cholesterol: 106 mg. • Sodium: 185 mg.
Exchanges: 3¼ very lean meat, 1½ vegetable, 3¼ fat

Rosemary-Garlic Quail with Baby Squash

2 tablespoons butter or
    margarine, melted
2 tablespoons olive oil
1 tablespoon snipped fresh
    rosemary
1 clove garlic, minced
    Salt and pepper to taste
4 whole dressed quail (4 to 6 oz.
    each), split in half, skin on
16 baby patty pan squash, halved
    (about 8 oz.)
16 baby zucchini squash, sliced
    lengthwise (about 7 oz.)

4 servings

Spray rack in broiler pan with nonstick vegetable cooking spray. Set aside. In small bowl, combine butter, oil, rosemary, garlic, salt and pepper. Brush both sides of quail halves and squash lightly with butter mixture. Arrange squash and quail halves skin-side-down on prepared pan.

Place pan under broiler with surface of quail 4 to 5 inches from heat. Broil for 12 to 15 minutes, or until meat is no longer pink and juices run clear, turning quail and squash and brushing with any remaining butter mixture once or twice.

Per Serving: Calories: 372 • Protein: 26 g. • Carbohydrate: 4 g. • Fat: 28 g.
• Cholesterol: 111 mg. • Sodium: 128 mg.
Exchanges: 3½ lean meat, ¾ vegetable, 3¼ fat

Apple-Apricot Quail Couscous

2 tablespoons vegetable oil
4 whole dressed quail (4 to 6 oz.
   each), split in half, skin on
2 cups apple juice
1 cup chopped tart red apple
1/3 cup chopped green onions
1/3 cup chopped dried apricots
1/3 cup dried currants
1 cup uncooked couscous*
1/4 cup pine nuts, toasted**

4 servings

In 12-inch nonstick skillet, heat oil over medium-high heat. Add quail halves. Cook for 4 to 6 minutes, or until browned, turning quail once. Remove quail from skillet. Wipe skillet with paper towels. Return quail to skillet.

Add juice. Bring to a boil over medium-high heat. Cover. Reduce heat to medium-low. Simmer for 10 to 15 minutes, or until meat is tender, turning quail once. Stir in apple, onions, apricots and currants. Simmer for 2 to 3 minutes, or until apple is tender-crisp. Remove quail from skillet. Set aside and keep warm.

Stir couscous into skillet. Bring to a boil. Cover. Remove from heat. Let stand for 4 to 5 minutes, or until liquid is absorbed. Stir in pine nuts. Place couscous on serving platter. Arrange quail halves on couscous.

Couscous is a Middle Eastern pasta made from granular durum wheat. It is a staple of North African cuisine.

**To toast pine nuts, place them in a dry skillet over medium-low heat until lightly browned, shaking pan occasionally.*

Per Serving: Calories: 658 • Protein: 34 g.
• Carbohydrate: 72 g. • Fat: 27 g.
• Cholesterol: 96 mg. • Sodium: 79 mg.
Exchanges: 2 1/4 starch, 3 1/2 lean meat, 2 1/2 fruit, 3 1/4 fat

Pineapple Quail Sauté ↑

1 tablespoon vegetable oil
4 whole dressed quail (4 to
   6 oz. each), split in half,
   skin on
1 can (20 oz.) pineapple
   chunks, drained (reserve
   3/4 cup liquid)
3/4 cup dry sherry

1/2 cup chopped red pepper
3 tablespoons chopped
   crystallized gingerroot
1 tablespoon soy sauce
3/4 teaspoon dry mustard
1 1/2 tablespoons cornstarch mixed
   with 1 1/2 tablespoons water
1/2 cup sliced green onions

4 servings

In 12-inch nonstick skillet, heat oil over medium-high heat. Add quail halves. Cook for 4 to 6 minutes, or until browned, turning quail once. Add reserved pineapple liquid, sherry, pepper, gingerroot, soy sauce and mustard. Cover. Simmer for 8 to 10 minutes, or until meat is no longer pink.

Stir in cornstarch mixture. Bring to a boil over medium-high heat. Cook for 1 to 2 minutes, or until sauce is thickened and glossy, stirring constantly. Stir in pineapple chunks and onions. Serve over hot cooked rice, if desired.

Per Serving: Calories: 478 • Protein: 26 g. • Carbohydrate: 39 g. • Fat: 19 g.
• Cholesterol: 96 mg. • Sodium: 339 mg.
Exchanges: 1/2 starch, 3 1/2 lean meat, 1 1/2 fruit, 1 3/4 fat

Peach-sauced Quail ↓

4 whole dressed quail (4 to 6 oz. each), skin on
1/3 cup cream sherry
2 tablespoons finely chopped onion
2 teaspoons grated fresh gingerroot
3/4 cup ready-to-serve chicken broth
1/4 teaspoon apple pie spice
1 cup peach purée*
2 tablespoons butter or margarine, melted

4 servings

Split each quail down the back, and flatten. (See Broiled Quail, page 58.) Spray rack in broiler pan with nonstick vegetable cooking spray. Arrange quail on prepared rack. Set aside.

In 2-quart saucepan, combine sherry, onion and gingerroot. Bring to a boil over medium-high heat. Boil for 3 to 4 minutes, or until liquid is nearly gone, stirring frequently. Stir in broth and pie spice. Bring to a boil. Boil for 8 to 9 minutes, or until liquid is reduced to 1/2 cup, stirring frequently. Stir in peach purée. Bring to a boil. Reduce heat to low. Simmer for 2 to 3 minutes, or until flavors are blended, stirring frequently. Remove from heat. Set sauce aside and keep warm.

Meanwhile, place quail under broiler with surface of meat 4 to 5 inches from heat. Broil for 12 to 15 minutes, or until meat is no longer pink and juices run clear, turning quail over and brushing with butter once or twice. Serve quail with warm sauce.

*To make peach purée, process frozen or peeled fresh peaches in food processor or blender until smooth.

Per Serving: Calories: 358 • Protein: 26 g. • Carbohydrate: 10 g. • Fat: 21 g.
• Cholesterol: 111 mg. • Sodium: 315 mg.
Exchanges: 3 1/2 lean meat, 1/2 fruit, 2 1/4 fat

Quail with Apricot Dressing

2 cups seasoned dried bread crumbs
1/2 cup chopped dried apricots
1/4 cup sliced celery
2 tablespoons chopped pecans
1 tablespoon snipped fresh parsley
1/4 teaspoon dried thyme leaves
1 1/3 cups ready-to-serve chicken broth
4 whole dressed quail (4 to 6 oz. each), skin on
1 tablespoon butter or margarine
Salt and pepper to taste
2 tablespoons orange-flavored liqueur
1 tablespoon sugar

4 servings

Heat oven to 400°F. In medium mixing bowl, combine crumbs, apricots, celery, pecans, parsley and thyme. Stir in chicken broth until dressing is evenly moistened. Spray 12 × 8-inch baking pan with nonstick vegetable cooking spray. Spoon dressing evenly over bottom of pan. Set aside.

Split each quail down the back, and flatten. (See Broiled Quail, page 58.) In 12-inch nonstick skillet, melt butter over medium-high heat. Add quail. Cook quail for 6 to 10 minutes, or until lightly browned, turning once. Arrange quail skin-side-up on dressing in baking pan. Season quail with salt and pepper. Cover with foil.

Bake for 20 minutes. In small bowl, combine liqueur and sugar. Brush quail with liqueur mixture. Bake, uncovered, for 5 to 10 minutes longer, or until meat is tender and juices run clear. Brush quail with any remaining mixture.

TIP: For a sweeter dressing, substitute corn bread crumbs for regular bread crumbs.

Per Serving: Calories: 593 • Protein: 35 g.
• Carbohydrate: 59 g. • Fat: 23 g.
• Cholesterol: 104 mg. • Sodium: 2027 mg.
Exchanges: 3 starch, 3 1/2 lean meat, 1/2 fruit, 2 1/4 fat

Oriental Grilled Quail

MARINADE:

¼ cup sliced green onions
3 tablespoons soy sauce
2 tablespoons honey
1 tablespoon sesame oil
1 tablespoon molasses
4 whole dressed quail (4 to 6 oz. each), deboned*, skin on

SALAD:

2 cups shredded Napa cabbage
½ medium red pepper, seeded and cut into 1 × ¼-inch strips
½ medium yellow pepper, seeded and cut into 1 × ¼-inch strips
1 small carrot, cut into 1 × ¼-inch strips (⅓ cup)

DRESSING:

3 tablespoons rice vinegar
1 teaspoon grated fresh gingerroot
1 teaspoon packed brown sugar
1 tablespoon sesame seed, toasted

4 servings

In shallow dish or sealable plastic bag, combine marinade ingredients. Place quail in marinade, turning to coat. Cover with plastic wrap, or seal bag. Chill 30 minutes.

In large mixing bowl or salad bowl, combine salad ingredients. In small bowl, whisk together dressing ingredients. Set salad and dressing aside.

Prepare grill for medium direct heat. Spray cooking grid with nonstick vegetable cooking spray. Drain and discard marinade from quail. Grill quail for 10 to 14 minutes, or until meat is no longer pink and juices run clear. Set aside and keep warm.

Pour dressing over salad. Toss to coat. Arrange salad evenly on individual serving plates. Top each salad with 1 quail. Sprinkle salads evenly with sesame seed.

To debone quail, split down the back, and flatten. Carefully cut out breast and back bones with tip of sharp knife. Do not remove bones in wings or legs.

Per Serving: Calories: 319 • Protein: 26 g. • Carbohydrate: 12 g. • Fat: 18 g. • Cholesterol: 96 mg. • Sodium: 462 mg.
Exchanges: 3½ lean meat, ¾ vegetable, 1½ fat

Dark–Small Birds

> ## Menu
>
> *Dove Breasts in Creamy Pepper Sauce (recipe below)*
>
> *Broiled Vegetable Mélange (recipe below)*
>
> *Crusty Italian Bread*

Dove Breasts in Creamy Pepper Sauce

3	tablespoons vegetable oil
4	tablespoons snipped fresh basil, divided
1	tablespoon lemon juice
1	teaspoon crushed red pepper flakes
1	clove garlic, minced
8	whole boneless skinless dove breasts (about 1 oz. each), split in half
2	tablespoons butter or margarine

1	medium red pepper, seeded and cut into strips
1	cup sliced fresh mushrooms
1/2	cup dry white wine
1/2	cup ready-to-serve chicken broth
1 1/2	cups half-and-half
2	tablespoons all-purpose flour
12	oz. uncooked linguine
1/2	cup shredded fresh Parmesan cheese

4 servings

In shallow dish, combine oil, 2 tablespoons basil, the juice, red pepper flakes and garlic. Add dove breast halves, stirring to coat. Cover with plastic wrap. Chill 1 to 2 hours, stirring occasionally.

In 12-inch skillet, melt 2 tablespoons butter over medium heat. Add pepper strips and mushrooms. Cook for 2 to 3 minutes, or until pepper is tender-crisp. Remove vegetables from skillet and set aside.

Add wine and broth to skillet. Bring to a boil over high heat. Boil for 4 to 6 minutes, or until liquid is reduced by half. Reduce heat to medium. In 2-cup measure, combine half-and-half and flour, stirring until smooth. Whisk mixture into skillet. Bring to a boil, stirring constantly. Stir in prepared vegetables. Set sauce aside and keep warm.

Prepare linguine as directed on package. Drain and discard marinade from breast halves. Spray rack in broiler pan with nonstick vegetable cooking spray. Arrange breast halves on rack. Place under broiler with surface of breast halves 4 to 5 inches from heat. Broil for 5 to 7 minutes, or until meat is no longer pink, turning breast halves once.

Arrange breast halves over prepared linguine. Stir remaining 2 tablespoons basil and the Parmesan cheese into sauce. Spoon sauce over dove breasts and linguine.

Per Serving: Calories: 757 • Protein: 32 g.• Carbohydrate: 74 g. Fat: 34 g.
• Cholesterol: 109 mg. • Sodium: 489 mg.
Exchanges: 4¼ starch, 2½ very lean meat, ½ vegetable, 6¾ fat

Broiled Vegetable Mélange

1	small eggplant
1	medium zucchini
1	small red onion, cut into 8 wedges
1	yellow or green pepper, seeded and sliced
2	tablespoons olive oil or herb-flavored oil

4 servings

Cut eggplant in half lengthwise, then cut crosswise into 1-inch slices. Cut zucchini in half lengthwise, then cut crosswise into 2-inch pieces. In large mixing bowl, combine all vegetables. Drizzle oil over vegetables, tossing to coat.

Spray rack in broiler pan with nonstick vegetable cooking spray. Arrange vegetables evenly on rack. Place under broiler with surface of vegetables 4 to 5 inches from heat. Broil for 5 to 10 minutes, or until vegetables are browned and tender-crisp, stirring occasionally.

TIP: Broil dove breasts and vegetables together on the same broiling pan. Cooking times will increase slightly, but it is more efficient.

Per Serving: Calories: 97 • Protein: 2 g.
• Carbohydrate: 9 g. • Fat: 7 g.
• Cholesterol: 0 mg. • Sodium: 7 mg.
Exchanges: 1¾ vegetable, 1¼ fat

Dove Risotto

3 cups ready-to-serve chicken broth
½ cup butter or margarine, divided
8 whole boneless skinless dove breasts (about 1 oz. each), cut into ½-inch pieces
8 oz. fresh or frozen asparagus, cut into 1-inch lengths
⅓ cup chopped red onion
1½ cups uncooked arborio rice
½ cup grated fresh Parmesan cheese

4 servings

In 1-quart saucepan, bring broth to a boil over high heat. Reduce heat to low to keep warm.

In 10-inch skillet, melt 3 tablespoons butter over medium-high heat. Add dove pieces, asparagus and onion. Cook for 4 to 6 minutes, or until meat is no longer pink, stirring occasionally. Set aside.

In 2-quart saucepan, melt 3 tablespoons butter over medium-high heat. Add rice. Cook for 2 minutes, stirring constantly. Stir in 1 cup hot broth. Cook, stirring constantly, until all liquid is absorbed. Continue adding broth, ½ cup at a time, as it is absorbed, stirring constantly until all broth is absorbed and rice is tender (about 20 minutes). Stir in dove mixture and remaining 2 tablespoons butter. Sprinkle Parmesan cheese over individual servings.

Per Serving: Calories: 644 • Protein: 26 g. • Carbohydrate: 63 g. • Fat: 31 g.
• Cholesterol: 123 mg. • Sodium: 1246 mg.
Exchanges: 3½ starch, 2 very lean meat, 2 vegetable, 6 fat

Dove Pastry Nests ↓

1 pkg. (10 oz.) frozen puff pastry shells, defrosted
1½ cups 1% milk
2 tablespoons all-purpose flour
2 tablespoons butter or margarine
8 whole boneless skinless dove breasts (about 1 oz. each), cut into ½-inch pieces
6 oz. fresh mushrooms, sliced (2 cups)
2 cloves garlic, minced
⅓ cup sliced green onions
1 medium carrot, shredded (⅓ cup)
2 to 4 tablespoons dry white wine (optional)
¼ teaspoon salt
¼ teaspoon pepper

6 servings

Bake puff pastry shells as directed on package. Set aside and keep warm.

In 2-cup measure, combine milk and flour. Stir until smooth. Set aside. In 12-inch skillet, melt butter over medium-high heat. Add dove pieces, mushrooms and garlic. Cook for 3 to 5 minutes, or until meat is lightly browned, stirring frequently. Stir flour mixture. Add to skillet. Bring to a boil, stirring constantly. Boil for 1 minute, stirring constantly. Stir in onions, carrot, wine, salt and pepper. Cook for 3 to 5 minutes, or until vegetables are tender-crisp, stirring constantly.

Remove tops from pastry shells. Spoon dove mixture evenly into shells. Lean top of shell against filled shell as garnish, if desired.

Per Serving: Calories: 393 • Protein: 15 g. • Carbohydrate: 29 g. • Fat: 24 g. • Cholesterol: 47 mg. • Sodium: 302 mg. Exchanges: 1½ starch, 1 very lean meat, ½ vegetable, ¼ low-fat milk, 4½ fat

Peach Doves & Rice

2 tablespoons butter or margarine
6 whole dressed doves (2 to 3 oz. each), skin on
1 cup ready-to-serve chicken broth
¼ cup chopped shallots
2 tablespoons brandy
¼ teaspoon salt
¼ teaspoon pepper
2 cups sliced fresh or frozen peaches
1 tablespoon cornstarch mixed with 2 tablespoons water
4 cups hot cooked white rice

4 servings

In 12-inch nonstick skillet, melt butter over medium-high heat. Add doves. Cook for 3 to 5 minutes, or until lightly browned, turning doves occasionally. Add broth, shallots, brandy, salt and pepper. Cover. Reduce heat to low. Simmer for 10 to 12 minutes, or until meat is nearly tender.

Add peaches to skillet. Cover. Cook for 5 to 10 minutes, or until meat is tender. Remove doves and peaches from skillet. Set aside and keep warm. Stir cornstarch mixture into skillet. Increase heat to medium-high. Cook for 1 to 2 minutes, or until sauce is thickened and glossy, stirring constantly. Serve doves and peaches over rice. Spoon sauce over top.

Per Serving: Calories: 640 • Protein: 22 g. • Carbohydrate: 70 g. • Fat: 27 g. • Cholesterol: 95 mg. • Sodium: 494 mg. Exchanges: 4 starch, 2¼ medium-fat meat, ½ fruit, 2¾ fat

Grilled Doves

MARINADE:

  2 tablespoons oil
  1 small onion, chopped (½ cup)
1½ cups catsup
  1 cup water
 ½ cup red wine vinegar
 ⅓ cup packed brown sugar
  3 tablespoons lemon juice
  2 tablespoons Worcestershire sauce
 ½ teaspoon pepper
 ¼ teaspoon dry mustard

  6 whole dressed doves (2 to 3 oz. each), skin on

4 servings

In 2-quart saucepan, heat oil over medium heat. Add onion. Cook for 2 to 3 minutes, or until onion is tender, stirring occasionally. Stir in remaining marinade ingredients. Bring to a boil over medium-high heat. Reduce heat to medium-low. Simmer for 15 to 20 minutes, or until marinade is slightly thickened. Remove from heat. Cool marinade completely.

Split each dove down the back, and flatten. Place doves in 9-inch square baking dish. Reserve ½ cup marinade; refrigerate. Pour remaining marinade over doves, turning doves to coat. Cover with plastic wrap. Refrigerate 8 hours or overnight, turning doves occasionally.

Prepare grill for medium direct heat. Spray cooking grid with nonstick vegetable cooking spray. Drain and discard marinade from doves. Arrange doves on cooking grid. Grill for 8 to 12 minutes, or until meat is no longer pink, turning doves and brushing with reserved marinade occasionally.

Per Serving: Calories: 370 • Protein: 17 g. • Carbohydrate: 24 g. • Fat: 24 g. • Cholesterol: 80 mg. • Sodium: 625 mg.
Exchanges: 2¼ medium-fat meat, 2½ fat

Dove Breast & Pear Salad  ↑

  5 cups water
  8 whole boneless skinless dove breasts (about 1 oz. each)
  4 cups mixed baby greens
  2 Seckel pears, cored and sliced*
  1 cup halved red seedless grapes
 ¼ cup sliced almonds, toasted
 ¼ cup sliced green onions
 ⅓ cup vegetable oil
 ¼ cup red wine vinegar
 ¼ cup pear nectar
  2 tablespoons honey

4 servings

In 2-quart saucepan, bring water to a boil over high heat. Add dove breasts. Return to a boil. Reduce heat to medium-low. Simmer for 4 to 5 minutes, or until meat is no longer pink. Drain and discard water from breasts. Cool breasts slightly. Cut into ½-inch strips. Set aside.

On individual serving plates, evenly arrange greens. Top greens evenly with pears, grapes and dove strips. Top evenly with almonds and onions. Set salads aside.

In 2-cup measure, combine oil, vinegar, nectar and honey. Whisk until smooth. Drizzle dressing evenly over salads.

To prevent pears from browning, rub cut sides with lemon juice.

Per Serving: Calories: 378 • Protein: 15 g. • Carbohydrate: 28 g. • Fat: 24 g. • Cholesterol: 51 mg. • Sodium: 49 mg.
Exchanges: 2 very lean meat, ½ vegetable, 1¼ fruit, 4¾ fat

Doves in Bread Dressing

2 tablespoons butter or
  margarine
8 whole boneless skinless dove
  breasts (about 1 oz. each),
  cut into ¹⁄₂-inch pieces
2 stalks celery, sliced (1 cup)
1 small onion, chopped (¹⁄₂ cup)
1 teaspoon poultry seasoning
¹⁄₄ teaspoon rubbed sage
¹⁄₄ teaspoon salt
¹⁄₄ teaspoon pepper
²⁄₃ cup 1% milk
2 eggs, beaten
8 cups cubed fresh bread
  (¹⁄₂-inch cubes)

SAUCE:

1 tablespoon butter or
  margarine
2 cups sliced fresh mushrooms
1¹⁄₂ cups 1% milk
2 tablespoons all-purpose flour
1 to 2 tablespoons dry sherry
1 teaspoon beef bouillon granules
¹⁄₄ to ¹⁄₂ teaspoon garlic powder
¹⁄₄ teaspoon salt
¹⁄₈ teaspoon pepper
1 tablespoon snipped
  fresh parsley

4 servings

Heat oven to 350°F. In 10-inch skillet, melt 2 tablespoons butter over medium heat. Add dove pieces, celery and onion. Cook for 3 to 5 minutes, or until meat is no longer pink, stirring occasionally. Stir in poultry seasoning, sage, salt and pepper. Set aside. In large mixing bowl, beat together ²⁄₃ cup milk and the eggs. Add bread cubes and dove mixture. Toss to combine.

Spray 8-inch square baking dish with nonstick vegetable cooking spray. Spoon bread mixture into dish. Cover with foil. Bake for 25 to 30 minutes, or until dressing is heated through.

Meanwhile, in 2-quart saucepan, melt 1 tablespoon butter over medium heat. Add mushrooms. Cook for 4 to 5 minutes, or until tender, stirring occasionally. In 2-cup measure, combine 1¹⁄₂ cups milk and the flour. Stir until smooth. Stir milk mixture into saucepan. Stir in remaining sauce ingredients, except parsley. Bring to a boil, stirring constantly. Boil for 1 minute, stirring constantly. Stir in parsley. Set aside and keep warm. Serve sauce with dressing.

Per Serving: Calories: 480 • Protein: 27 g. • Carbohydrate: 50 g. • Fat: 18 g.
• Cholesterol: 187 mg. • Sodium: 1103 mg.
Exchanges: 2¹⁄₂ starch, 2¹⁄₂ lean meat, 1¹⁄₄ vegetable, ¹⁄₂ low-fat milk, 1¹⁄₂ fat

Woodcock Rumaki ↓

*Because of its liverlike flavor, woodcock makes an ideal
substitute in this classic liver appetizer.*

- 1 tablespoon vegetable oil
- 1 lb. boneless skinless woodcock meat, cut into
  1½-inch pieces
- 1 tablespoon soy sauce
- 1 tablespoon dry sherry
- 1 teaspoon lemon juice
- 1 teaspoon grated fresh gingerroot
- 1 clove garlic, minced
- 12 slices bacon, cut in half crosswise
- 12 whole water chestnuts, halved

24 appetizers

In 12-inch nonstick skillet, heat oil over medium-low
heat. Add woodcock pieces. Cook for 2 to 3 minutes,
or until meat is no longer pink, stirring occasionally.
Remove from heat. Add soy sauce, sherry, juice,
gingerroot and garlic to skillet. Toss to coat. Cool
completely.

Top 1 piece bacon with 1 piece woodcock and
1 water chestnut half. Roll bacon around woodcock
and water chestnut; secure with wooden pick. Repeat
with remaining bacon, woodcock and water chestnuts. Drizzle rumaki with pan drippings. Cover with
plastic wrap. Chill at least 2 hours, turning rumaki
over occasionally.

Arrange rumaki on rack in broiler pan. Place under
broiler with surface of rumaki 4 to 5 inches from
heat. Broil for 12 to 15 minutes, or until bacon is
crisp, turning rumaki over occasionally.

Per Serving: Calories: 55 • Protein: 6 g. • Carbohydrate: 1 g.
• Fat: 3 g. • Cholesterol: 15 mg. • Sodium: 101 mg.
Exchanges: ¾ very lean meat,
¼ vegetable, ½ fat

Spicy Stir-fried Woodcock

MARINADE:

- 1 tablespoon soy sauce
- 2 teaspoons oyster sauce
- 2 teaspoons sesame oil
- 1 clove garlic, minced
- 1 teaspoon sugar
- 1 teaspoon rice vinegar
- ½ teaspoon cornstarch
- ¼ teaspoon five-spice powder
- ¼ teaspoon crushed red pepper flakes

- 8 oz. boneless skinless woodcock meat, cut into
  2 × ¼-inch strips
- 1 teaspoon vegetable oil
- 4 oz. fresh mushrooms, sliced (1½ cups)
- ½ cup red pepper strips
- ¼ cup sliced green onions
- 2 cups hot cooked white rice

2 servings

In medium mixing bowl, combine marinade ingredients. Add woodcock strips, stirring to coat. Let stand
for 15 minutes, stirring occasionally.

In 12-inch nonstick skillet or wok, heat oil over
medium-high heat. Add mushrooms, pepper and
onions. Cook for 2 to 3 minutes, or until vegetables
are tender-crisp, stirring constantly. Remove vegetables from skillet; set aside.

Add meat mixture to skillet. Cook for 2 to 3 minutes,
or until meat is no longer pink, stirring constantly.
Stir in vegetables. Serve mixture over rice.

Per Serving: Calories: 527 • Protein: 35 g. • Carbohydrate: 68 g.
• Fat: 12 g. • Cholesterol: 75 mg. • Sodium: 804 mg.
Exchanges: 3½ starch, 3½ very lean meat, 1 vegetable, 2¼ fat

Woodcock Pâté ↓

2 tablespoons butter
1 cup finely chopped shallots
½ cup dry white wine
8 oz. pork back fat*
8 oz. boneless skinless woodcock
   meat, ground and crumbled
8 oz. ground pork, crumbled
8 oz. ground veal, crumbled
1 egg
1 tablespoon all-purpose flour
½ cup finely chopped ham
¼ cup whole pistachios
3 tablespoons cognac or brandy

SPICE MIX:
  2 teaspoons salt
  1 teaspoon pepper
½ teaspoon ground allspice
½ teaspoon ground coriander
½ teaspoon ground ginger
¼ teaspoon ground nutmeg

12 oz. bacon strips
  Hot water

8 servings

In 10-inch skillet, melt butter over medium heat. Add shallots. Cook for 4 to 5 minutes, or until shallots are golden, stirring occasionally. Add wine. Bring to a simmer. Simmer for 8 to 10 minutes, or until wine is reduced by two-thirds. Transfer shallots to large mixing bowl. Cool completely.

In food processor, process back fat until smooth, scraping sides of bowl occasionally. Remove half of back fat; set aside. Add half of woodcock, half of pork and half of veal to processor. Process until smooth. Transfer meat mixture to mixing bowl with shallots. Repeat with remaining back fat, woodcock, pork and veal. Add egg and flour to mixing bowl. Mix well. Add ham, pistachios, cognac and spice mix to mixing bowl. Mix well.

Heat oven to 350°F. Line bottom and sides of 9 × 5-inch loaf dish with bacon strips, reserving 4 strips and cutting strips to fit. Spoon meat mixture into prepared dish, pressing to eliminate air pockets. Cover evenly with remaining bacon. Cover tightly with foil.

Place loaf dish in 13 × 9-inch baking dish. Pour hot water into baking dish halfway up sides of loaf dish. Carefully place in oven. Bake for 2 hours. Remove from oven, and let loaf cool to room temperature in water bath. Pour excess liquid off top of pâté; re-cover.

To firm texture of pâté, weight it down by placing a second loaf pan on top. Fill the pan with 1 to 2 lbs. of canned goods. Secure cans with rubber bands or masking tape. Refrigerate at least 24 hours and up to 3 days. Unmold pâté. Remove and discard bacon. Cut pâté into ½-inch slices for a first course served with tiny dill pickles (cornichons), slice it thin and cut it into wedges to serve on crackers, or use it as sandwich meat.

Back fat is the pure white fat from pork. It has no seasonings and has not been cured. Ask the meat cutter at the supermarket or a meat market to provide you with back fat.

TIP: Pâté's flavor is best when it is served at room temperature.

Per Serving: Calories: 556 • Protein: 21 g. • Carbohydrate: 6 g. • Fat: 48 g.
• Cholesterol: 133 mg. • Sodium: 806 mg.
Exchanges: 3 high-fat meat, ½ vegetable, 4½ fat

Goose

Menu

Roast Goose (recipe below) ❧ *Winter Fruit Dressing (recipe below)*
Twice-baked Potatoes ❧ *Steamed Green Beans*

Roast Goose

1 tablespoon all-purpose flour
1 whole dressed goose (about
   8 lbs.), skin on
1 cup dry red wine
1 cup water
1 pkg. (1 oz.) onion soup mix

6 to 8 servings

Heat oven to 350°F. Add flour to turkey-size (23½ × 19-inch) oven cooking bag; shake to distribute. Place cooking bag in large roasting pan.

Rinse goose and pat dry with paper towels. Place goose in oven cooking bag. In small mixing bowl, combine wine, water and soup mix. Pour mixture over goose in bag. Secure bag with provided nylon tie. Insert meat thermometer into thickest part of goose breast through top of bag. Make six ½-inch slits in top of bag.

Roast goose for 1½ to 2 hours, or until internal temperature registers 180°F. Remove goose from bag. Let stand, tented with foil, for 10 minutes before carving.

Per Serving: Calories: 662 • Protein: 54 g.
• Carbohydrate: 1 g. • Fat: 47 g.
• Cholesterol: 196 mg. • Sodium: 231 mg.
Exchanges: 7¾ medium-fat meat, 1½ fat

Winter Fruit Dressing

2 tablespoons butter or margarine
1 stalk celery, sliced (½ cup)
¼ cup chopped onion
6 cups cubed whole-grain bread
   (½-inch cubes)
2 cups chopped mixed dried fruit
   (apples, apricots, cranberries,
   raisins)
1 to 1½ cups ready-to-serve
   chicken broth
½ cup pecan halves
½ teaspoon rubbed sage leaves
½ teaspoon dried rosemary leaves
¼ teaspoon dried thyme leaves
   Salt and pepper to taste

6 to 8 servings

In medium skillet, melt butter over medium heat. Add celery and onion. Cook for 2 to 3 minutes, or until vegetables are tender-crisp.

In large mixing bowl, combine celery mixture, bread cubes and dried fruit. Stir in enough broth to just moisten mixture. Stir in remaining ingredients. Mix well.

Spray 2-quart casserole with nonstick vegetable cooking spray. Spoon dressing into casserole. Cover. Bake in 350°F oven with goose for 40 to 45 minutes, or until heated through. For a crisp top on dressing, uncover during last 15 minutes of baking.

Per Serving: Calories: 226 • Protein: 4 g. • Carbohydrate: 35 g. • Fat: 9 g.
• Cholesterol: 8 mg. • Sodium: 337 mg.
Exchanges: 1 starch, 1¼ fruit, 1¾ fat

Orange & Chili Glazed Goose

1 whole dressed goose (about 8 lbs.), skin on
4 sprigs fresh rosemary
3 tablespoons grated fresh orange peel
½ cup chili sauce
¼ cup frozen orange juice concentrate, defrosted
¼ cup honey
2 teaspoons snipped fresh rosemary leaves
¼ cup water

6 to 8 servings

Heat oven to 350°F. Rinse goose and pat dry with paper towels. Loosen skin over breast to form a pocket. Stuff rosemary sprigs and peel under skin. Place goose breast-side-up on rack in roasting pan.

In small mixing bowl, combine chili sauce, concentrate, honey and snipped rosemary. Brush goose with ¼ of glaze mixture. Pour water into bottom of roasting pan. Cover with foil.

Roast for 45 minutes. Remove foil. Roast for 1 to 1½ hours longer, or until internal temperature in thickest part of breast registers 180°F, basting with remaining glaze every 15 minutes. Let stand, tented with foil, for 10 minutes before carving.

Per Serving: Calories: 710 • Protein: 55 g. • Carbohydrate: 13 g. • Fat: 47 g.
• Cholesterol: 196 mg. • Sodium: 323 mg.
Exchanges: 7¾ medium-fat meat, ½ fruit, 1½ fat

Apricot-glazed Goose

1 whole dressed goose (about
   8 lbs.), skin on
½ cup ready-to-serve chicken
   broth or water
⅓ cup apricot preserves
¼ cup apricot-flavored brandy
¼ cup chopped dried apricots
2 tablespoons honey
2 tablespoons frozen orange juice
   concentrate, defrosted

6 to 8 servings

Heat oven to 350°F. Rinse goose
and pat dry with paper towels. Place
goose breast-side-up on rack in
roasting pan. Pour broth into bottom of pan. Cover with foil. Roast
for 1 hour.

Meanwhile, in 1-quart saucepan,
combine remaining ingredients.
Bring to a boil over medium heat,
stirring constantly. Boil for 1 minute, stirring constantly. Reserve
⅓ cup glaze for basting. Set
remaining glaze aside and keep
warm.

Remove foil. Roast for 50 to 60
minutes longer, or until internal
temperature in thickest part of
breast registers 180°F, basting
with reserved glaze every
10 minutes during last
30 minutes. Let stand,
tented with foil, for
10 minutes before
carving. Serve
with remaining
glaze.

Per Serving:
Calories: 745
• Protein: 55 g.
• Carbohydrate:
  19 g.
• Fat: 47 g.
• Cholesterol:
  196 mg.
• Sodium: 219 mg.
Exchanges: 7¾
medium-fat meat,
¼ fruit, 1¾ fat

Fruit-braised Goose Breast ↓

1 whole bone-in goose breast
   (2 to 3 lbs.), skin on
1½ cups dry white wine
1½ cups apricot nectar
½ cup coarsely chopped prunes
½ cup coarsely chopped dried
   apples
½ cup coarsely chopped
   dried figs

4 to 6 servings

Place goose breast in 6-quart Dutch oven. Add wine, nectar, prunes,
apples and figs. Bring to a boil over high heat. Cover. Reduce heat to
medium-low. Simmer for 1½ to 2 hours, or until meat is tender.

Heat oven to 375°F. Place breast skin-side-up on rack in roasting pan. Set
aside. Strain mixture in Dutch oven through fine-mesh sieve. Set fruit
aside and keep warm. Skim fat off strained liquid, if desired. Place liquid
in 1-quart saucepan. Bring to a boil over high heat. Boil for 10 to 12 minutes, or until sauce is reduced to 1 cup.

Brush goose breast with some of the sauce. Roast breast for 15 to 20 minutes, or until browned, brushing occasionally with sauce. Serve breast
with reserved fruit and any remaining sauce.

Per Serving: Calories: 699 • Protein: 26 g. • Carbohydrate: 33 g. • Fat: 52 g.
• Cholesterol: 123 mg. • Sodium: 126 mg.
Exchanges: 3¾ high-fat meat, 2 fruit, 4½ fat

Smoked Goose

Smoked goose makes a great appetizer when served with a variety of spicy dips, such as a barbecue sauce or mustard sauce. It can also add a smoky flavor to other recipes like soups.

BRINE:

6 cups water

½ cup plus 2 tablespoons canning/pickling salt

½ cup plus 2 tablespoons packed brown sugar

3 tablespoons maple syrup

2 tablespoons plus 1 teaspoon white vinegar

2 teaspoons pickling spice

1 whole dressed goose (about 8 lbs.), skin on
Hickory wood chips

¼ cup honey

1 tablespoon soy sauce

⅛ to ¼ teaspoon cayenne
Hot water or chicken broth

25 2-oz. servings

In large nonmetallic container, combine brine ingredients. Stir until salt and sugar are dissolved. Add goose. Cover. Refrigerate overnight, turning goose once or twice. Drain and discard brine from goose. Pat goose dry with paper towels. Let goose air dry for 45 minutes.

While goose is air drying, heat water smoker or insulated smoker to 200°F. Soak wood chips in warm water for 30 minutes; drain. In small bowl, combine honey, soy sauce and cayenne. Brush goose with honey mixture. Place goose on rack in middle position of smoker. Place pan ⅔ full of hot water on rack directly under goose*. Place a handful of wood chips in smoker.

Smoke goose for 8 to 10 hours, or until internal temperature in thickest part of breast registers 180°F, adding wood chips once or twice.

*Pan of water is for catching dripping fat from goose, and the steam from the water keeps the goose from getting too dry.

Per Serving: Calories: 225 • Protein: 17 g. • Carbohydrate: 4 g. • Fat: 15 g.
• Cholesterol: 63 mg. • Sodium: 342 mg.
Exchanges: 2½ medium-fat meat, ½ fat

Currant-Mustard Goose Breast

- 1 whole bone-in goose breast (2 to 3 lbs.), skin on
- 1/2 teaspoon salt
- 1/4 teaspoon pepper
- 2 tablespoons vegetable oil
- 1/2 cup currant jelly
- 2 tablespoons Dijon mustard

4 to 6 servings

Heat oven to 350°F. Sprinkle goose breast evenly with salt and pepper. Line 13 × 9-inch roasting pan with foil. Place breast skin-side-up in pan. Brush breast evenly with oil. Cover with foil. Roast for 1 hour.

In small bowl, combine jelly and mustard. Remove foil. Brush half of jelly mixture over breast. Roast, uncovered, for 40 to 50 minutes, or until internal temperature in thickest part of breast registers 180°F. Brush with remaining jelly mixture. Let stand, tented with foil, for 10 minutes before carving.

TIP: Lining the pan with foil makes cleanup easy.

Per Serving: Calories: 509 • Protein: 33 g.
• Carbohydrate: 18 g. • Fat: 33 g.
• Cholesterol: 118 mg. • Sodium: 402 mg.
Exchanges: 4 1/2 medium-fat meat, 2 fat

Goose Jerky LOW-FAT →

MARINADE:
- 2 cups cold water
- 1 can (5.5 oz.) spicy vegetable juice
- 1/4 cup soy sauce
- 1/4 cup Worcestershire sauce
- 1 to 2 tablespoons Morton® TenderQuick® mix
- 2 teaspoons onion powder
- 1/2 teaspoon garlic powder
- 1/2 teaspoon ground ginger

- 2 lbs. boneless skinless goose meat, cut into 4 × 1 × 1/4-inch strips
  Hickory wood chips

11 servings (40 to 50 slices)

Per Serving: Calories: 136 • Protein: 19 g.
• Carbohydrate: 1 g. • Fat: 6 g.
• Cholesterol: 69 mg. • Sodium: NA
Exchanges: 2 1/2 very lean meat, 1 fat

In large nonmetallic bowl or sealable plastic bag, combine marinade ingredients. Stir to dissolve TenderQuick mix. Add goose strips, stirring to coat. Cover with plastic wrap, or seal bag. Refrigerate 24 hours, stirring or turning bag occasionally.

Soak wood chips in warm water for 30 minutes; drain. Heat smoker to 120°F. Spray smoker racks with nonstick vegetable cooking spray. Drain and discard marinade from goose strips. Pat strips lightly with paper towels. Arrange strips at least 1/4 inch apart on prepared racks. Place racks in smoker.

Place a handful of wood chips in smoker. Smoke goose strips for 3 to 6 hours, or until jerky is dry but not brittle, adding wood chips as necessary and keeping smoker temperature at 120°F. Cool jerky completely. Store jerky, loosely wrapped, in refrigerator for 1 week, or wrap tightly and freeze up to 2 months.

OVEN METHOD: Add 2 teaspoons liquid smoke flavoring to marinade. Continue with recipe as directed, except omit wood chips. Heat oven to lowest possible temperature setting, propping oven door with wooden spoon if necessary to maintain 120°F. Spray cooling racks with nonstick vegetable cooking spray. Arrange goose strips on prepared racks, spacing as directed. Dry strips in oven for 3 to 4 hours, or until dry but not brittle.

Oriental Barbecued Goose Kabobs

MARINADE:

1/4 cup dry sherry

1/4 cup hoisin sauce

3 tablespoons Chinese plum sauce

2 tablespoons Chinese black bean sauce

3 cloves garlic, minced

2 teaspoons grated fresh gingerroot

1 lb. boneless skinless goose meat, cut into 1-inch cubes

1 can (20 oz.) pineapple chunks, drained (32 chunks)

6 green onions, cut into 1 1/2-inch lengths (24 pieces)

1 medium green pepper, seeded and cut into 1 1/2-inch pieces (16 pieces)

8 skewers (10-inch)

4 cups hot cooked white rice

4 servings

In medium mixing bowl, combine marinade ingredients. Reserve 1/4 cup marinade; set aside. Add goose to remaining marinade, stirring to coat. Cover with plastic wrap. Chill 2 to 4 hours, stirring occasionally.

Prepare grill for medium direct heat. Spray cooking grate with nonstick vegetable cooking spray. Thread goose cubes, pineapple chunks, onion pieces and pepper pieces evenly on skewers.

Arrange kabobs on prepared grate. Grill, covered, for 7 to 8 minutes, or until meat is desired doneness, turning kabobs two or three times. Brush kabobs with reserved 1/4 cup marinade during last 2 minutes of cooking time. Serve kabobs over rice.

Per Serving: Calories: 601 • Protein: 33 g.
• Carbohydrate: 85 g. • Fat: 12 g.
• Cholesterol: 85 mg. • Sodium: 551 mg.
Exchanges: 3 1/2 starch, 3 1/4 lean meat, 1 fruit, 1/2 fat

Goose Cacciatore *LOW-FAT* →

2 tablespoons butter or margarine
8 oz. fresh mushrooms, quartered
1 medium onion, sliced
2 cloves garlic, minced
1 can (28 oz.) whole tomatoes, cut up
2 cups (8 oz.) chopped cooked goose
1/2 cup dry red wine
1 1/2 teaspoons dried Italian seasoning
1/2 teaspoon pepper
1/2 teaspoon salt
6 cups hot cooked rice

6 servings

In 4-quart saucepan, melt butter over medium heat.
Add mushrooms, onion and garlic. Cook for 5 to 6
minutes, or until vegetables are tender, stirring occasionally. Stir in remaining ingredients, except rice.

Bring to a boil over medium-high heat. Cover.
Reduce heat to medium-low. Simmer for 45 minutes
to 1 hour, or until goose is tender, stirring occasionally. Serve goose mixture over rice.

Per Serving: Calories: 440 • Protein: 19 g. • Carbohydrate: 68 g.
• Fat: 10 g. • Cholesterol: 47 mg. • Sodium: 478 mg.
Exchanges: 3 1/2 starch, 1 1/4 lean meat, 3 vegetable, 1 fat

Goose Pot Pie

1/2 cup water
1 pkg. (16 oz.) frozen mixed
    vegetables
1 1/2 cups (8 oz.) cubed processed
    American cheese (1/2-inch
    cubes)
1 cup (4 oz.) chopped cooked
    goose
1/2 cup slivered red onion
1/4 teaspoon pepper

CRUST:
2 cups all-purpose flour
1 teaspoon salt
3/4 cup vegetable shortening
1 tablespoon vinegar
2 to 3 tablespoons cold water

6 servings

Heat oven to 425°F. In 2-quart saucepan, bring 1/2 cup water to a boil over
high heat. Add vegetables. Cook for 3 to 5 minutes, or until vegetables are
tender-crisp, stirring occasionally. Drain. Return vegetables to saucepan.
Add cheese. Cook over low heat, stirring until cheese melts. Stir in goose,
onion and pepper. Set aside.

In medium mixing bowl, combine flour and salt. Using pastry blender, cut
in shortening until particles resemble coarse crumbs. Add vinegar. Mix well.
Sprinkle with water, 1 tablespoon at a time, mixing with fork until particles
are moistened and cling together. Shape dough into ball. Cover ball with
plastic wrap. Chill 15 minutes. Divide dough in half. On lightly floured
surface, roll half of dough into 12-inch circle. Fit circle into 9-inch pie plate.

Spoon goose mixture into prepared pie plate. On lightly floured surface, roll
remaining dough into 11-inch circle. Cut vents in circle with sharp knife.
Place circle over goose mixture. Roll edges of bottom and top crusts together.
Flute edges or press together with tines of fork to seal. Bake at 425°F for 15
minutes. Reduce heat to 350°F. Bake for 20 to 25 minutes longer, or until
filling is bubbly and crust is browned. Let stand for 10 minutes before serving.

TIP: Substitute refrigerated pie crust or your favorite 2-crust pie crust for
the one used in this recipe, if desired.

Per Serving: Calories: 629 • Protein: 21 g. • Carbohydrate: 46 g. • Fat: 41 g.
• Cholesterol: 54 mg. • Sodium: 960 mg.
Exchanges: 3 starch, 2 high-fat meat, 5 fat

Zesty Goose & Rice Casserole

This is a very easy recipe that can be prepared in a hurry. It's a great way to use leftovers.

3 cups cooked brown rice
2 cups frozen corn kernels, defrosted
2 cups grated sharp Cheddar cheese
1½ cups (6 oz.) cubed cooked goose (½-inch cubes)
1½ cups 1% milk
1 small onion, finely chopped (¾ cup)
1 jar (2 oz.) diced pimiento, drained
1 tablespoon chili powder
¼ teaspoon cayenne

4 to 6 servings

Heat oven to 350°F. In large mixing bowl, combine all ingredients. Mix well. Spray 3-quart casserole with nonstick vegetable cooking spray. Spoon mixture into prepared casserole. Bake for 40 to 50 minutes, or until bubbly around edges. Let stand for 5 minutes before serving.

Per Serving: Calories: 438 • Protein: 27 g. • Carbohydrate: 40 g. • Fat: 20 g. • Cholesterol: 78 mg. • Sodium: 315 mg. Exchanges: 2¼ starch, 2½ medium-fat meat, ¼ vegetable, ¼ low-fat milk, 1 fat

Oriental Goose Salad VERY FAST ↓

⅔ cup rice vinegar
2 tablespoons hoisin sauce
1 tablespoon teriyaki sauce
½ teaspoon five-spice powder
⅓ cup sesame oil
4 cups mixed baby greens
1 cup (4 oz.) shredded cooked goose
1 cup quartered fresh mushrooms
½ cup slivered red onion
½ cup snow pea pods
⅓ cup carrot strips (2 × ¼-inch strips)

4 servings

In food processor or blender, combine vinegar, hoisin sauce, teriyaki sauce and five-spice powder. Process until blended. With processor running, gradually add oil in slow drizzle until well blended. Set dressing aside.

In large mixing bowl or salad bowl, combine greens, goose, mushrooms, onion, pea pods and carrot strips. Drizzle dressing over salad. Toss to combine.

Per Serving: Calories: 293 • Protein: 11 g.
• Carbohydrate: 14 g. • Fat: 22 g.
• Cholesterol: 27 mg. • Sodium: 373 mg.
Exchanges: 1 lean meat, 2½ vegetable, 3½ fat

Curried Goose & Spinach VERY FAST

This recipe follows traditional Indian cooking techniques. It combines a variety of spices for a curry that is fresher tasting than one made with prepared curry powder.

2 tablespoons peanut oil
1½ lbs. boneless skinless goose meat, cut into 1-inch cubes
½ teaspoon ground turmeric
⅛ teaspoon ground allspice
2 tablespoons vegetable oil
1 to 2 jalapeño peppers, seeded and chopped
½ teaspoon fennel seed, crushed
½ teaspoon coriander seed, crushed
½ teaspoon cumin seed, crushed
1 bay leaf
12 cups coarsely torn fresh spinach, stems removed
1 teaspoon maple syrup
½ teaspoon salt
1 tablespoon fresh lime or lemon juice
Hot cooked Basmati rice (optional)
Lime or lemon wedges

4 to 6 servings

In 12-inch skillet or wok, heat peanut oil over medium-high heat. Add goose. Cook for 4 to 6 minutes, or until meat is no longer pink, stirring frequently. Drain goose on paper-towel-lined plate. Sprinkle goose with turmeric and allspice, tossing to coat. Set aside.

Wipe out skillet. In same skillet, heat vegetable oil over medium heat. Add jalapeños, fennel, coriander, cumin and bay leaf. Cook for 1 minute, stirring constantly. Add spinach, syrup and salt. Cook for 1 to 1½ minutes, or just until spinach is wilted, stirring constantly. Add goose and juice. Toss to combine. Cook for 1 to 2 minutes, or until heated through, stirring constantly. Remove and discard bay leaf. Serve goose mixture over rice with lime wedges.

Per Serving: Calories: 275 • Protein: 29 g. • Carbohydrate: 6 g.
• Fat: 15 g. • Cholesterol: 95 mg. • Sodium: 371 mg.
Exchanges: 3½ very lean meat, 1 vegetable, 3 fat

Goose Salad Sandwiches ↓

This easy but flavorful goose salad can easily be doubled or tripled. Use it as a sandwich filling, or serve it on a lettuce-lined plate with tomato wedges.

- 1 cup (4 oz.) chopped cooked goose
- ⅓ cup sliced pimiento-stuffed green olives
- ¼ cup mayonnaise
- 3 tablespoons sliced green onions
  Freshly ground pepper to taste
- 4 slices whole-grain bread
- 1 medium tomato, sliced
- 2 lettuce leaves

2 servings

In small mixing bowl, combine goose, olives, mayonnaise, onions and pepper. Cover with plastic wrap. Refrigerate several hours or overnight to allow flavors to blend.

Spread goose salad evenly over 2 slices of bread. Top each with tomato slices, lettuce leaf and second slice of bread.

Per Serving: Calories: 515 • Protein: 23 g.
• Carbohydrate: 31 g. • Fat: 34 g.
• Cholesterol: 71 mg. • Sodium: 1045 mg.
Exchanges: 2 starch, 2 lean meat,
¾ vegetable, 5 fat

Barbecued Goose Sandwiches

1 tablespoon vegetable oil
1 small onion, chopped (½ cup)
3 cups (12 oz.) shredded cooked goose
1 cup water
½ cup catsup
½ cup chili sauce
1 tablespoon packed brown sugar
1 tablespoon Worcestershire sauce
2 teaspoons dry mustard
2 teaspoons fresh horseradish
½ to 1 teaspoon red pepper sauce
¼ teaspoon garlic powder
¼ teaspoon salt
6 to 8 onion buns, split

6 to 8 servings

In 3-quart saucepan, heat oil over medium heat. Add onion. Cook for 3 to 4 minutes, or until tender, stirring occasionally. Stir in remaining ingredients, except buns. Bring to a simmer. Reduce heat to medium-low. Simmer for 15 to 20 minutes, or until meat is tender and mixture is desired thickness. Serve barbecued goose on buns.

TIP: Add tomato or pickle slices to sandwiches, if desired.

Per Serving: Calories: 290 • Protein: 17 g. • Carbohydrate: 34 g.
• Fat: 10 g. • Cholesterol: 41 mg. • Sodium: 782 mg.
Exchanges: 1½ starch, 1½ lean meat,
½ vegetable, 1 fat

Moroccan Goose Couscous

This dish can be made in a hurry for a light, but satisfying, meal. Serve it at room temperature with a tossed salad and some bread.

1 cup uncooked couscous*
2 cups (8 oz.) shredded cooked goose
½ cup sliced green onions
⅓ cup chopped walnuts
⅓ cup raisins
3 tablespoons honey
2 tablespoons butter or margarine, melted
¼ teaspoon ground cinnamon
⅛ teaspoon ground ginger
⅛ teaspoon ground cumin
    Dash pepper
    Dash ground cloves

4 servings

Prepare couscous as directed on package. In large mixing bowl or serving bowl, combine prepared couscous and remaining ingredients. Mix well.

Couscous is a Middle Eastern pasta made from granular durum wheat. It is a staple of North African cuisine.

Per Serving: Calories: 511 • Protein: 24 g. • Carbohydrate: 61 g.
• Fat: 19 g. • Cholesterol: 70 mg. • Sodium: 112 mg.
Exchanges: 2¾ starch, 2 lean meat, ½ fruit, 2½ fat

Smoky Split Pea & Goose Soup 🔵 LOW-FAT

- 6 cups water
- 1 lb. dried split peas, rinsed and drained
- 4 cups ready-to-serve chicken broth
- 2 cups (8 oz.) cubed smoked goose (1/4-inch cubes)
- 2 cups sliced leeks
- 2 cups cubed peeled russet potatoes (1/4-inch cubes)
- 1 1/2 cups cubed carrots (1/4-inch cubes)
- 1/2 teaspoon salt
- 1/4 teaspoon pepper
  Red pepper sauce to taste (optional)

10 servings

In 6-quart Dutch oven, combine water and peas. Bring to a boil over high heat. Boil for 2 minutes. Remove from heat. Cover. Let stand for 1 hour.

Add broth, goose and leeks to split peas. Bring to a boil over medium-high heat. Cover. Reduce heat to medium-low. Simmer for 45 minutes. Stir in potatoes and carrots. Re-cover. Simmer for 15 to 20 minutes, or until vegetables are tender and peas are creamy. Stir in salt, pepper and red pepper sauce.

TIP: The flavor of this soup actually improves after a day or two in the refrigerator.

Per Serving: Calories: 301 • Protein: 20 g. • Carbohydrate: 39 g. • Fat: 8 g. • Cholesterol: 25 mg. • Sodium: 665 mg. Exchanges: 2 starch, 1 1/2 medium-fat meat, 1 3/4 vegetable

Smoked Goose & Vegetable Soup 🔵 LOW-FAT ↑

- 4 cups ready-to-serve chicken broth, divided
- 2 medium carrots, sliced (1 cup)
- 1 stalk celery, sliced (1/2 cup)
- 3 cloves garlic, minced
- 2 cups (8 oz.) cubed smoked goose (1/4-inch cubes)
- 2 cups chopped white cabbage
- 1 can (16 oz.) whole tomatoes, cut up
- 1 can (8 oz.) tomato sauce
- 3/4 teaspoon dried basil leaves
- 1/2 teaspoon pepper
- 1 can (15 oz.) red beans, rinsed and drained

8 servings

In 4-quart Dutch oven, combine 2 cups broth, the carrots, celery and garlic. Bring to a boil over medium-high heat. Reduce heat to medium. Cook for 5 to 7 minutes, or until vegetables are tender-crisp, stirring occasionally.

Stir in remaining ingredients, except beans. Bring to a boil over medium-high heat, stirring occasionally. Cover. Reduce heat to low. Simmer for 1 to 1 1/2 hours, or until vegetables and goose are tender, stirring occasionally. Stir in beans. Cook for 4 to 6 minutes, or until heated through, stirring occasionally.

Per Serving: Calories: 199 • Protein: 14 g. • Carbohydrate: 15 g. • Fat: 9 g. • Cholesterol: 31 mg. • Sodium: 1016 mg. Exchanges: 1/2 starch, 1 1/4 medium-fat meat, 1 3/4 vegetable, 1/2 fat

Spanish Rice & Goose Casserole

- 1 pkg. (6.8 oz.) Spanish rice mix
- 2 teaspoons olive oil
- 3/4 lb. ground goose*, crumbled
- 1 can (15 oz.) black beans, rinsed and drained
- 1 can (14 1/2 oz.) diced tomatoes with chilies, undrained
- 1/2 cup sliced green onions
- 2 teaspoons chili powder
- 1 teaspoon ground cumin
- 1/8 teaspoon cayenne (optional)
- 1 cup shredded Colby-Jack cheese
  Sour cream for garnish (optional)

6 servings

Heat oven to 375°F. Prepare rice as directed on package. Meanwhile, in 12-inch nonstick skillet, heat oil over medium heat. Add goose. Cook for 3 to 5 minutes, or until meat is no longer pink, stirring occasionally. Remove from heat. Drain.

Add prepared rice and remaining ingredients, except cheese and sour cream, to skillet. Mix well. Spoon mixture into 2-quart casserole. Cover. Bake for 25 to 30 minutes, or until hot and bubbly around edges. Uncover. Sprinkle evenly with cheese. Bake for 5 to 10 minutes longer, or until cheese is melted. Garnish with sour cream.

Grind goose through a meat grinder, finely chop it with a knife or process it in a food processor until desired texture.

Per Serving: Calories: 375 • Protein: 23 g.
• Carbohydrate: 33 g. • Fat: 16 g.
• Cholesterol: 64 mg. • Sodium: 1149 mg.
Exchanges: 2 starch, 2 1/2 very lean meat, 1/2 vegetable, 3 fat

Goose Lasagna Casserole ↓

This easy lasagna casserole can be made to your liking with the pasta sauce of your choice.

- 3/4 lb. ground goose*, crumbled
- 1 small onion, chopped (1/2 cup)
- 2 cloves garlic, minced
- 1 jar (26 oz.) prepared pasta sauce
- 1 1/2 teaspoons dried Italian seasoning (optional)
- 2 1/2 cups uncooked mini lasagna noodles
- 1 1/2 cups cottage cheese
- 1 1/2 cups shredded part-skim mozzarella cheese, divided
  Fresh parsley for garnish (optional)

6 servings

Heat oven to 375°F. Spray 12 × 8-inch baking dish with nonstick vegetable cooking spray. Set aside. In 2-quart saucepan, combine goose, onion and garlic. Cook over medium heat for 6 to 7 minutes, or until meat is no longer pink, stirring occasionally. Drain. Stir in sauce and Italian seasoning. Cook for 10 minutes to blend flavors, stirring occasionally.

Meanwhile, prepare noodles as directed on package. Drain. In large mixing bowl, combine noodles, sauce mixture, cottage cheese and 1 cup mozzarella cheese. Spoon mixture into prepared baking dish. Cover with foil.

Bake for 25 minutes. Uncover. Sprinkle remaining mozzarella cheese evenly over top. Bake for 10 to 15 minutes longer, or until cheese is melted and lightly browned. Let stand for 5 minutes before serving. Garnish with parsley.

Grind goose through a meat grinder, finely chop it with a knife or process it in a food processor until desired texture.

Per Serving: Calories: 448 • Protein: 32 g. • Carbohydrate: 41 g. • Fat: 17 g.
• Cholesterol: 72 mg. • Sodium: 1010 mg.
Exchanges: 1 1/4 starch, 3 1/2 medium-fat meat, 2 vegetable

Puddle Ducks

Menu

Ducks with Orange Sauce (recipe below)
Potato Galette with Chive Sour Cream (recipe below)
Crusty French Bread ❧ Tossed Baby Greens with Vinaigrette

Ducks with Orange Sauce

   1 medium orange
   2 whole dressed puddle ducks (1¼ to 1½ lbs. each),
      skin on
   1 small onion, quartered
   2 whole cloves garlic
   ¼ cup butter, melted
   2 teaspoons dried rosemary leaves
   1 teaspoon dried thyme leaves
   1 teaspoon dried parsley flakes
   ⅔ cup ready-to-serve chicken broth
   ½ cup orange-flavored liqueur
   ¼ cup orange juice
   1 tablespoon red wine vinegar

4 servings

Heat oven to 400°F. With vegetable peeler, peel
1 tablespoon orange zest from orange. (Do not include
white part of orange.) Set zest aside. Cut orange
into quarters.

Stuff ducks evenly with orange quarters, onion and
garlic cloves. Secure legs with kitchen string. Tuck
wing tips behind back. Place ducks breast-side-up
on rack in roasting pan. Brush evenly with butter.
Sprinkle ducks evenly with rosemary, thyme and
parsley. Roast for 35 to 45 minutes, or until skin is
golden brown and meat is desired doneness. Place
ducks on serving platter. Set aside and keep warm.

Pour pan juices into 10-inch skillet. Stir in broth,
liqueur, juice and zest. Bring to a boil over medium-
high heat. Boil for 8 to 10 minutes, or until liquid is
reduced to ½ cup, stirring occasionally. Stir in vinegar. Simmer for 3 minutes. Serve sauce with ducks.

Per Serving: Calories: 563 • Protein: 34 g. • Carbohydrate: 15 g.
• Fat: 40 g. • Cholesterol: 181 mg. • Sodium: 391 mg.
Exchanges: 4½ medium-fat meat, ½ vegetable, 3½ fat

Potato Galette with Chive Sour Cream

   ¼ cup sour cream
   2 tablespoons finely chopped onion
   1 tablespoon snipped fresh chives
   2 teaspoons lemon juice
   3 medium russet potatoes, peeled and grated
      (2½ cups)
   ¼ cup butter, melted, divided
      Salt and pepper to taste

4 servings

In small bowl, combine sour cream, onion, chives
and juice. Set aside.

Heat oven to 400°F. In medium mixing bowl, combine potatoes and 2 tablespoons butter. Toss to coat.
Stir in salt and pepper. Heat 10-inch ovenproof skillet over high heat. Add remaining 2 tablespoons
butter to skillet and swirl to coat. Add potatoes to
skillet, pressing to flatten potatoes into one pancake.

Cook over high heat for 2 minutes. Reduce heat to
medium. Cook for 2 to 4 minutes longer, or until
bottom of galette is golden brown. Turn galette over
by inverting onto a plate, then sliding it back into
skillet. Cook for 4 to 5 minutes, or until second side
is golden brown.

Place skillet in oven. Bake galette for 12 to 15
minutes, or until crisp. Serve galette with chive
sour cream.

Per Serving: Calories: 211 • Protein: 2 g. • Carbohydrate: 18 g.
• Fat: 15 g. • Cholesterol: 37 mg. • Sodium: 133 mg.
Exchanges: 1¼ starch, 3 fat

Traditional Roast Duck with Dressing

DRESSING:

- 6 cups cubed dry bread (1/2-inch cubes)
- 3 tablespoons butter or margarine
- 8 oz. fresh mushrooms, sliced (3 cups)
- 1 stalk celery, sliced (1/2 cup)
- 1 small onion, chopped (1/2 cup)
- 2 to 3 teaspoons poultry seasoning
- 1/2 teaspoon salt
- 1/4 teaspoon dried thyme leaves
- 1/4 teaspoon freshly ground pepper
- 1/4 cup ready-to-serve chicken broth

- 1 teaspoon salt
- 1 teaspoon caraway seed, crushed
- 1/4 teaspoon freshly ground pepper
- 2 whole dressed puddle ducks (1 1/4 to 1 1/2 lbs. each), skin on
- 1 medium onion, quartered
- 2 tablespoons butter, melted

4 servings

Heat oven to 400°F. Place bread in large mixing bowl. Set aside. In 10-inch skillet, melt butter over medium heat. Add mushrooms, celery and onion. Cook for 3 to 5 minutes, or until vegetables are tender-crisp, stirring occasionally. Add vegetables, poultry seasoning, salt, thyme and pepper to bread. Stir to combine. Add broth. Toss just until moistened. (Do not overmix.)

Spray 1 1/2-quart casserole with nonstick vegetable cooking spray. Spoon dressing into casserole. Cover. Place in oven. (Dressing should bake 40 to 45 minutes, or until very hot.)

In small bowl, combine salt, caraway seed and pepper. Sprinkle mixture evenly over surface and in cavities of ducks. Place ducks breast-side-up in 12 × 8-inch baking dish. Place ducks in oven with dressing. Bake for 30 minutes. Reduce temperature to 350°F. Brush ducks with butter. Bake for 15 to 30 minutes longer, or until meat is desired doneness. Let ducks stand for 10 minutes before cutting. Serve ducks with dressing.

TIP: If desired, uncover dressing during last 15 minutes of baking to brown top.

Per Serving: Calories: 710 • Protein: 39 g. • Carbohydrate: 36 g. • Fat: 45 g. • Cholesterol: 189 mg. • Sodium: 1437 mg.
Exchanges: 1 3/4 starch, 4 1/2 medium-fat meat, 1 3/4 vegetable, 4 1/2 fat

Grill-smoked Duck

BRINE:

- 6 cups cold water
- ½ cup plus 1 tablespoon canning/pickling salt
- ¼ cup plus 2 tablespoons packed brown sugar
- 3 tablespoons maple syrup
- 2 tablespoons plus 1 teaspoon white vinegar
- 2 teaspoons pickling spice

- 1 whole dressed puddle duck (1¼ to 1½ lbs.), skin on
  Hickory wood chips
- 2 tablespoons honey
- 2 teaspoons soy sauce
  Hot chicken broth, beer or water

3 to 4 servings

In large nonmetallic bowl or sealable plastic bag, combine brine ingredients. Stir until salt and sugar are dissolved. Add duck. Cover. Refrigerate 4 hours, turning duck once or twice. Drain and discard brine from duck. Pat duck dry with paper towels. Let duck air dry for 30 minutes.

While duck is air drying, start large load of charcoal briquettes on one side of charcoal grill. Soak wood chips in warm water for 30 minutes; drain. In small bowl, combine honey and soy sauce. When briquettes are covered with light ash, toss a handful of wood chips on them. Place pan ⅔ full of hot broth on cooking grid over charcoal. Brush duck with honey mixture and place it on opposite side of cooking grid. Cover grill.

Smoke duck for 3 to 4 hours, or until internal temperature in thickest part of breast registers at least 160°F. (Do not open grill unless necessary.) Temperature in grill should stay between 150° and 200°F. Regulate temperature using vents on grill. Add more wood chips during last hour of smoking.

TIP: See thermometer tip with Grill-smoked Pheasant, page 18.

Per Serving: Calories: 239 • Protein: 16 g. • Carbohydrate: 11 g. • Fat: 14 g. • Cholesterol: 75 mg. • Sodium: 667 mg.
Exchanges: 2¼ medium-fat meat, ½ fat

Cranberry-Jalapeño Glazed Duck Breast ↓

1 pkg. (8 oz.) fresh or frozen cranberries
1 cup water
3/4 cup sugar
1/2 cup dried cranberries
1/4 cup finely chopped onion

1 jalapeño pepper, seeded and chopped
2 boneless puddle duck breasts (6 to 8 oz. each), split in half, skin on
Orange zest twists, for garnish

4 servings

In 2-quart saucepan, combine fresh cranberries, water and sugar. Bring to a boil over high heat. Reduce heat to medium-low. Simmer for 4 to 6 minutes, or until cranberries pop, stirring occasionally. Strain mixture through fine-mesh sieve, pressing cranberries to extract juice. Discard cranberry pulp and wash saucepan.

Return strained cranberry juice to saucepan. Stir in dried cranberries, onion and jalapeño. Bring to a boil over high heat. Reduce heat to medium-low. Simmer for 5 minutes to blend flavors. Remove glaze from heat.

Heat oven to 350°F. Spray 9-inch baking dish with nonstick vegetable cooking spray. Place duck breasts skin-side-up in prepared pan. Pour glaze evenly over breasts. Cover with foil. Bake for 25 minutes. Uncover. Bake for 5 to 8 minutes longer, or until meat is desired doneness, spooning glaze over breasts every 2 minutes.

Arrange breasts on serving platter. Spoon some glaze from dish over and around breasts. Garnish with orange zest twists.

Per Serving: Calories: 310 • Protein: 20 g. • Carbohydrate: 56 g. • Fat: 1 g.
• Cholesterol: 104 mg. • Sodium: 105 mg.
Exchanges: 2¾ very lean meat, 1 fruit

Duck Breasts with Whiskey-Peppercorn Sauce

SAUCE:
1 tablespoon butter
3 tablespoons finely chopped shallots or onion
1 1/2 cups ready-to-serve beef broth
1/2 cup dry white wine
1/4 cup plus 1 tablespoon sour-mash whiskey, divided
2 to 3 teaspoons coarsely ground pepper
1/4 cup heavy whipping cream
1/4 teaspoon salt

1/2 teaspoon coarse salt
2 boneless skinless puddle duck breasts (6 to 8 oz. each), split in half
2 tablespoons butter

4 servings

In 2-quart saucepan, melt 1 tablespoon butter over medium heat. Add shallots. Cook for 2 to 3 minutes, or until golden brown, stirring frequently. Stir in broth, wine, 1/4 cup whiskey and the pepper. Bring to a boil over medium-high heat. Boil for 10 to 15 minutes, or until reduced by half, stirring occasionally. Stir in cream. Continue boiling for 8 to 10 minutes, or until sauce reduces to 1 cup, stirring frequently. Stir in remaining 1 tablespoon whiskey and 1/4 teaspoon salt. Set sauce aside and keep warm.

Sprinkle coarse salt evenly in bottom of 10-inch nonstick skillet. Heat skillet over medium-high heat. Add duck breasts. Cook for 2 to 3 minutes, or until browned, turning breasts over once. Reduce heat to medium-low. Add 2 tablespoons butter to skillet. Cook for 4 to 5 minutes, or until meat is desired doneness. Spoon sauce over or around duck breasts on serving plates.

Per Serving: Calories: 253 • Protein: 21 g.
• Carbohydrate: 6 g. • Fat: 15 g.
• Cholesterol: 148 mg. • Sodium: 826 mg.
Exchanges: 2¾ very lean meat, 3 fat

Tea-smoked Duck FAST

This unusual preparation of duck involves smoking it in a wok on your stove. Don't worry—it won't smoke up your kitchen, and cleanup is a breeze.

2 boneless puddle duck breasts (6 to 8 oz. each), split in half, skin on
½ teaspoon seasoned salt
⅛ teaspoon cayenne
1 tablespoon peanut oil

SMOKING MIXTURE:
¼ cup loose black tea leaves
¼ cup packed brown sugar
¼ cup uncooked white rice
1 tablespoon whole peppercorns
1 cinnamon stick, broken
1 tablespoon fresh orange peel strips (1 × ¼-inch strips)

4 servings

Sprinkle duck breasts evenly with salt and cayenne. In 12-inch non-stick skillet, heat oil over medium-high heat until very hot. Cook breasts in skillet for 5 to 7 minutes, or just until golden, turning breasts over once. Set aside.

Line wok with heavy-duty foil, leaving 3 inches of overlap around edges. In small mixing bowl, combine all smoking mixture ingredients. Spread mixture in bottom of wok. Spray wok rack or small round cooling rack with nonstick vegetable cooking spray. Place rack in wok about 1½ inches above smoking mixture. Arrange duck breasts on rack.

Heat wok over high heat. When smoking mixture begins to smoke, place lid on wok and fold foil over edge of lid to seal. Smoke for 4 minutes. Remove wok from heat. Let stand for 3 minutes. Slowly remove lid. Serve smoked breasts on a bed of steamed or stir-fried vegetables, if desired.

TIP: To almost eliminate smoke in kitchen, remove wok lid under stove vent hood with fan running.

Per Serving: Calories: 239 • Protein: 17 g. • Carbohydrate: 0 g. • Fat: 18 g. • Cholesterol: 79 mg. • Sodium: 213 mg. Exchanges: 2½ medium-fat meat, 1 fat

Horseradish-Ginger Duck Breasts ↑

1 cup fresh sourdough bread crumbs
2 tablespoons grated fresh horseradish
1 tablespoon grated fresh gingerroot
¼ teaspoon salt
⅛ teaspoon white pepper
¼ cup butter or margarine, melted
2 green onions, thinly sliced
2 boneless skinless puddle duck breasts (6 to 8 oz. each), split in half

4 servings

In medium mixing bowl, combine crumbs, horseradish, gingerroot, salt and pepper. Add butter. Mix until crumbs soften and form a paste. Stir in green onions. Set aside.

Spray rack in broiler pan with nonstick vegetable cooking spray. Arrange duck breasts on rack. Place under broiler with surface of breasts 4 to 5 inches from heat. Broil for 3 to 5 minutes, or until meat is almost to desired doneness. Turn breasts over. Spoon crumb mixture evenly onto breasts, patting mixture to form a crust. Broil for 2 to 3 minutes, or until crumbs are lightly browned.

Per Serving: Calories: 238 • Protein: 21 g. • Carbohydrate: 10 g. • Fat: 12 g. • Cholesterol: 135 mg. • Sodium: 427 mg. Exchanges: ½ starch, 2¾ very lean meat, ¼ vegetable, 2½ fat

Sweet & Sour Duck

This traditional Chinese recipe may seem labor-intensive, but it produces especially crisp pieces of duck.

1 egg, beaten
3 tablespoons cornstarch, divided
1 tablespoon vegetable oil
1 teaspoon soy sauce
1/2 teaspoon salt
1/4 teaspoon white pepper
2 boneless skinless puddle duck breasts (6 to 8 oz. each), cut into 3/4-inch pieces
   Vegetable oil

FLOUR MIXTURE:
1/3 cup all-purpose flour
1/3 cup water
1/2 teaspoon salt
1/2 teaspoon baking soda

SAUCE:
1/2 cup packed brown sugar
1/3 cup white vinegar
3 tablespoons cornstarch
2 teaspoons soy sauce
1 can (81/4 oz.) unsweetened pineapple chunks, drained (reserve liquid)
1 cup (4 oz.) trimmed fresh snow pea pods
1/4 cup sliced green onions
4 cups hot cooked white rice

4 servings

In medium mixing bowl, combine egg, 2 tablespoons cornstarch, 1 tablespoon oil, 1 teaspoon soy sauce, 1/2 teaspoon salt and the pepper. Add duck pieces, stirring to coat. Cover with plastic wrap. Refrigerate at least 30 minutes, stirring occasionally.

Pour oil into wok to 1-inch depth. Heat oil over medium-high heat to 350°F. In medium mixing bowl, combine flour mixture ingredients. Stir duck pieces in flour mixture until well coated. Cook half of duck pieces in wok for 3 to 4 minutes, or until light brown, turning pieces frequently. Drain pieces on paper-towel-lined plate. Repeat with remaining duck pieces.

Increase oil temperature to 375°F. Return all duck pieces to wok at once. Fry for 1 to 2 minutes, or until golden brown, turning pieces frequently. Drain pieces on paper-towel-lined plates. Set duck aside and keep warm.

In 1-quart saucepan, combine all sauce ingredients. In 1-cup measure, combine reserved pineapple liquid and enough water to equal 1 cup. Add to saucepan. Cook over medium-high heat for 3 to 5 minutes, or until mixture is thickened and bubbly, stirring constantly. Stir in pineapple chunks and pea pods. Cook for 1 minute, stirring contantly.

In serving bowl, combine duck pieces and sauce mixture. Sprinkle onions over top. Serve over rice.

TIP: Let oil reheat before frying second batch of duck pieces.

Per Serving: Calories: 774 • Protein: 29 g. • Carbohydrate: 119 g. • Fat: 20 g. • Cholesterol: 157 mg. • Sodium: 1100 mg.
Exchanges: 3 3/4 starch, 2 1/2 medium-fat meat, 1/2 vegetable, 1/2 fruit, 1 1/2 fat

Five-spice Duck Stir-fry

SAUCE:

- 2 tablespoons soy sauce
- 1 tablespoon dry sherry
- 2 teaspoons cornstarch
- 1/8 teaspoon cayenne

- 1/4 cup roasted rice powder*
- 1/2 teaspoon five-spice powder
- 1/4 teaspoon salt
- 1/8 teaspoon cayenne
- 2 boneless skinless puddle duck breasts (6 to 8 oz. each), cut into 3/4-inch pieces
- 2 tablespoons sesame oil, divided
- 2 cloves garlic, minced
- 2 cups sliced bok choy
- 1 medium red pepper, cut into 2 × 1/4-inch slivers (1 cup)
- 1/2 cup sliced green onions (2-inch lengths)
- 1/2 cup carrot slivers (2 × 1/4-inch slivers)
- 4 cups hot cooked white rice

4 servings

In small bowl, combine sauce ingredients. Set aside. In sealable plastic bag, combine rice powder, five-spice powder, salt and cayenne. Add duck pieces. Seal bag; shake to coat.

Heat 12-inch nonstick skillet or wok over medium-high heat. Add 1 tablespoon oil and swirl for 15 seconds. Add duck pieces. Cook for 2 1/2 to 3 minutes, or until browned, stirring constantly. Remove duck from wok and set aside.

To same skillet, add remaining 1 tablespoon oil and swirl for 15 seconds. Add garlic. Cook for 30 seconds, stirring constantly. Add bok choy, red pepper, onions and carrot. Cook for 2 to 3 minutes, or until vegetables are tender, stirring constantly. Stir sauce ingredients and add to skillet. Cook for 15 to 30 seconds or until sauce is thickened and translucent, stirring constantly. Stir duck pieces into skillet. Cook for 1 minute to heat through, stirring constantly. Serve over rice.

To make roasted rice powder, spread 1/4 cup white rice in single layer on baking sheet. Bake at 375°F for 15 to 18 minutes, or until golden brown, shaking pan once or twice. Process rice in blender until powdered.

TIP: Stir-frying goes very fast, so have all ingredients prepared before starting to cook.

Per Serving: Calories: 506 • Protein: 28 g. • Carbohydrate: 77 g. • Fat: 8 g.
• Cholesterol: 104 mg. • Sodium: 789 mg.
Exchanges: 3 starch, 2 3/4 very lean meat, 2 vegetable, 1 1/2 fat

Sun-dried Tomato Duck Breasts

½ cup snipped drained oil-pack sun-dried tomatoes
¼ cup shredded fresh Parmesan cheese
3 cloves garlic, minced
1 teaspoon dried basil leaves
2 boneless puddle duck breasts (6 to 8 oz. each),
　　split in half, skin on
　Salt and pepper to taste

4 servings

Heat oven to 375°F. In small bowl, combine tomatoes, Parmesan cheese, garlic and basil. Set aside.

Spray baking sheet with nonstick vegetable cooking spray. Arrange duck breasts on prepared baking sheet. Sprinkle breasts evenly with salt and pepper to taste. Bake for 15 to 18 minutes, or until meat is desired doneness, spreading tomato mixture evenly over breasts during last 5 minutes of cooking.

Per Serving: Calories: 295 • Protein: 24 g. • Carbohydrate: 12 g.
• Fat: 18 g. • Cholesterol: 109 mg. • Sodium: 232 mg.
Exchanges: 3 medium-fat meat, 1½ vegetable, ½ fat

Hot & Sour Duck Soup ↓

Sesame oil adds a distinct and nutty flavor to this easy soup.

4 cups ready-to-serve chicken broth
¼ cup rice wine vinegar
2 tablespoons soy sauce
1 tablespoon cornstarch
1 cup (4 oz.) cooked puddle duck strips
　　(1 × ½ × ¼-inch strips)
⅓ cup sliced fresh shiitake mushrooms
¼ cup shredded carrot
¼ cup sliced green onions
½ teaspoon sesame oil
¼ teaspoon white pepper

4 servings

In 2-quart saucepan, combine broth, vinegar, soy sauce and cornstarch. Bring to a boil over medium-high heat, stirring constantly. Stir in remaining ingredients. Cook for 4 to 5 minutes, or until heated through, stirring occasionally.

Per Serving: Calories: 120 • Protein: 10 g. • Carbohydrate: 5 g.
• Fat: 6 g. • Cholesterol: 28 mg. • Sodium: 1539 mg.
Exchanges: 1 lean meat, 1 vegetable, ¾ fat

Creamy Wild Rice-Duck Soup →

This easy recipe is a great way to use leftover wild rice and duck meat.

   3 tablespoons butter or margarine
 ½ cup finely chopped carrot
 ½ cup thinly sliced celery
 ¼ cup finely chopped onion
 ⅓ cup all-purpose flour
   3 cups ready-to-serve chicken
      broth
   2 cups cooked wild rice
   2 cups half-and-half
 ⅓ cup dry white wine
 ¼ teaspoon salt
 ¼ teaspoon pepper
 ⅛ teaspoon ground nutmeg
   1 cup (4 oz.) cubed cooked
      puddle duck (¼-inch cubes)

6 servings

In 3-quart saucepan, melt butter over medium-high heat. Add carrot, celery and onion. Cook for 5 to 7 minutes, or until vegetables are tender, stirring occasionally. Stir in flour. Cook for 1 minute, stirring constantly. Blend in broth, stirring until smooth. Bring to a boil.

Stir in rice, half-and-half, wine, salt, pepper and nutmeg. Cook for 8 to 10 minutes, or until hot, stirring constantly. (Do not boil.) Stir in duck. Cook for 2 to 3 minutes, or until heated through, stirring constantly.

Per Serving: Calories: 310 • Protein: 12 g. • Carbohydrate: 22 g. • Fat: 19 g. • Cholesterol: 64 mg. • Sodium: 710 mg. Exchanges: 1½ starch, ¾ lean meat, ¼ vegetable, 3 fat

Oriental Duck Soup

   5 cups ready-to-serve chicken
      broth
1½ cups (6 oz.) cubed cooked
      puddle duck (½-inch cubes)
   1 medium carrot, shredded
      (½ cup)
 ½ cup sliced green onions (1-inch
      pieces)
   2 oz. cellophane noodles
      (bean threads), cut into
      thirds
   1 teaspoon soy sauce
 ⅓ cup chopped peanuts or
      cashews

4 servings

In 3-quart saucepan, bring broth to a boil over medium-high heat. Stir in duck, carrot, onions, noodles and soy sauce. Cook for 4 to 5 minutes, or until noodles are tender, stirring frequently.

Sprinkle individual servings evenly with nuts. Serve with additional soy sauce, if desired.

Per Serving: Calories: 267 • Protein: 18 g. • Carbohydrate: 17 g. • Fat: 14 g. • Cholesterol: 44 mg. • Sodium: 1377 mg. Exchanges: 1 starch, 1¾ lean meat, ½ vegetable, 1¾ fat

Smoked Duck Hash Packets

This recipe takes a little effort to prepare, but the time spent is well worth it. Guaranteed to be a big hit.

2 tablespoons butter or margarine
½ cup finely chopped onion
½ cup finely chopped celery
1 cup finely chopped tart green apple
½ cup finely chopped spicy Cajun sausage (Andouille)
1 cup (4 oz.) finely chopped smoked puddle duck
½ cup finely chopped carrot
3 tablespoons all-purpose flour
1 cup ready-to-serve chicken broth
2 tablespoons dry sherry
½ teaspoon rubbed sage
¼ teaspoon dried thyme leaves
¼ teaspoon salt
⅛ teaspoon pepper

SAUCE:
3 medium tart green apples, peeled and chopped (3½ cups)
¼ cup water
3 tablespoons brandy, divided
2 tablespoons packed brown sugar
1 tablespoon butter
1 pkg. (17¼ oz.) frozen puff pastry dough, defrosted
1 egg beaten with 2 tablespoons milk

6 servings

In 12-inch nonstick skillet, melt butter over medium heat. Add onion and celery. Cook for 2 minutes, stirring frequently. Stir in 1 cup apple and the sausage. Increase heat to medium-high. Cook for 2 minutes, stirring frequently. Stir in duck and carrot.

Stir in flour. Cook for 1 minute, stirring constantly. Blend in broth, sherry, sage, thyme, salt and pepper. Bring to a boil. Cook for 3 to 4 minutes, or until carrot is tender and liquid is reduced, stirring frequently. Set filling aside to cool.

In 2-quart saucepan, combine apples, water and 2 tablespoons brandy. Bring to a boil over medium-high heat. Reduce heat to medium-low. Cover. Simmer for 8 to 10 minutes, or until apples are tender, stirring occasionally. Stir in brown sugar, butter and remaining 1 tablespoon brandy. Set sauce aside and keep warm.

Heat oven to 450°F. On lightly floured surface, roll 1 pastry sheet into 12 × 8-inch rectangle. Cut dough into six 4-inch squares. Brush edges of squares with egg mixture. Spoon 3 rounded tablespoons filling into center of each square. Fold two opposite corners of squares over filling to meet in middle. Fold remaining two corners to middle to form peaks, pinching ends and seams to seal. Brush packets with egg mixture. Repeat with remaining dough and filling.

Spray baking sheet with nonstick vegetable cooking spray. Arrange packets on baking sheet. Bake for 14 to 16 minutes, or until packets are golden brown. Serve packets with warm sauce.

TIP: For more color, add finely chopped red pepper to filling with duck and carrot.

Per Serving: Calories: 780 • Protein: 16 g. • Carbohydrate: 65 g. • Fat: 49 g. • Cholesterol: 88 mg. • Sodium: 875 mg.
Exchanges: 2¾ starch, 1 medium-fat meat, 1 vegetable, ¾ fruit, 8½ fat

Duck Risotto →

6 cups ready-to-serve chicken broth
2 tablespoons olive oil
1 small onion, thinly sliced
2 cloves garlic, minced
2 cups uncooked arborio rice*
3/4 cup dry white wine
3 cups shredded fresh spinach
2 cups (8 oz.) chopped cooked puddle duck
1 medium tomato, seeded and coarsely chopped (1 cup)
1/2 cup halved pitted Kalamata olives
  Salt and pepper to taste
1/4 cup snipped fresh parsley

8 servings

In 2-quart saucepan, bring broth to a simmer over medium heat. Keep hot. In 6-quart Dutch oven, heat oil over medium heat. Add onion and garlic. Cook for 3 to 4 minutes, or until onion is tender, stirring occasionally. Add rice. Cook for 3 minutes, stirring constantly. Add wine. Cook for 3 to 4 minutes, or until wine is evaporated, stirring frequently.

Add 1/2 cup broth to rice. Cook, stirring constantly, until broth is absorbed. Continue adding broth and cooking in this manner for 30 to 35 minutes, or until all broth is absorbed and rice is tender and creamy, stirring constantly. During last 5 minutes of cooking, stir in spinach, duck, tomato, olives, salt and pepper. Stir in parsley just before serving.

*Arborio rice is a short, fat Italian rice. Its high starch content is what gives risotto such a creamy texture.

TIP: Substitute one chopped roasted red pepper for tomato, if desired.

Per Serving: Calories: 338 • Protein: 13 g.
• Carbohydrate: 44 g. • Fat: 11 g.
• Cholesterol: 28 mg. • Sodium: 944 mg.
Exchanges: 2 1/4 starch, 1 lean meat, 2 vegetable, 1 1/2 fat

Fresh Duck Sausage

3/4 lb. ground puddle duck breast and thighs*, crumbled
3/4 lb. ground pork or veal, crumbled
3 tablespoons cold water
2 teaspoons salt

1/2 teaspoon rubbed sage
1/2 teaspoon ground thyme
1/4 to 1/2 teaspoon white pepper
1/8 teaspoon ground ginger
  Dash ground nutmeg

6 servings

In medium mixing bowl, combine duck and pork. Mix well. In small bowl, combine remaining ingredients. Add spice mixture to meat mixture. Mix by hand until ingredients are evenly distributed.

Shape meat mixture into twelve 3-inch patties. Panfry or grill patties. To freeze patties, layer them between sheets of wax paper. Stack patties, wrap in foil and freeze no longer than 2 months.

*To grind duck, cut breast and thighs into 1-inch pieces, then grind through 3/16-inch plate on meat grinder.

Per Serving: Calories: 203 • Protein: 20 g. • Carbohydrate: <1 g. • Fat: 13 g.
• Cholesterol: 75 mg. • Sodium: 790 mg.
Exchanges: 3 lean meat, 3/4 fat

Blackberry-Duck Salad ↑

DRESSING:

- ³/₄ cup frozen blackberries, defrosted
- ¹/₄ cup raspberry white wine vinegar
- ¹/₄ cup sugar
- 2 tablespoons sour cream
- 1 tablespoon Dijon mustard
- 1 clove garlic, minced
- 1 cup vegetable oil

- 4 cups mixed baby salad greens
- 1¹/₂ cups sliced fresh or frozen peaches
- ¹/₂ cup sliced red onion
- 2 cups (8 oz.) sliced or shredded cooked puddle duck
  Fresh blackberries for garnish (optional)

4 servings

Place frozen blackberries in fine-mesh sieve over bowl. Press berries with back of spoon to release ¹/₂ cup juice. Discard pulp and seeds. In blender or food processor, combine blackberry juice, vinegar, sugar, sour cream, mustard and garlic. Process until smooth. With blender running, gradually add oil in slow drizzle until well blended. Chill dressing.

In large mixing bowl, combine greens, peaches and onion. Toss to combine. Arrange greens mixture evenly on individual serving plates. Mound ¹/₂ cup duck in center of each serving plate. Garnish with blackberries. Serve with dressing.

Per Serving: Calories: 745 • Protein: 17 g. • Carbohydrate: 29 g.
• Fat: 63 g. • Cholesterol: 60 mg. • Sodium: 153 mg.
Exchanges: 2¹/₄ lean meat, 1¹/₄ vegetable, ³/₄ fruit, 11¹/₄ fat

Wood Duck with Apples & Apricots

- 2 whole dressed wood ducks (¹/₂ to ³/₄ lb. each), skin on
- 1 medium red apple, cored and chopped (1 cup)
- ¹/₂ cup apricot preserves
- ¹/₂ cup apple cider
- ¹/₄ cup chopped dried apricots
- ¹/₄ teaspoon ground cloves

2 servings

Heat oven to 400°F. Secure legs of ducks with kitchen string. Place ducks on rack in roasting pan. Roast, uncovered, for 15 minutes.

Meanwhile, in 1-quart saucepan, combine apple, preserves, cider, dried apricots and cloves. Bring to a boil over high heat. Reduce heat to medium-low. Simmer for 2 to 3 minutes, or until apple is tender but not mushy, stirring occasionally. Reserve ³/₄ cup sauce. Set aside and keep warm.

Reduce oven temperature to 350°F. Roast ducks for 20 to 30 minutes longer, or until meat is desired doneness, brushing ducks with remaining sauce every 5 minutes. Serve ducks with reserved sauce.

Per Serving: Calories: 654 • Protein: 31 g. • Carbohydrate: 77 g.
• Fat: 26 g. • Cholesterol: 136 mg. • Sodium: 131 mg.
Exchanges: 4¹/₄ medium-fat meat, 2 fruit, 1 fat

Sautéed Wood Duck with Balsamic-Date Sauce LOW-FAT ↓

SAUCE:

¾ cup water
⅓ cup chopped dates
2 tablespoons balsamic vinegar
4 boneless skinless wood duck breasts (3 to 4 oz. each), split in half
    Salt and pepper to taste
1 tablespoon butter or margarine
1 small onion, sliced

4 servings

In 1-quart saucepan, combine sauce ingredients. Bring to a boil over high heat, stirring occasionally. Reduce heat to low. Simmer for 12 to 15 minutes, or until sauce is desired thickness, stirring occasionally. Set aside and keep warm.

Sprinkle duck breasts evenly with salt and pepper to taste. In 10-inch skillet, melt butter over medium heat. Add breasts and onion. Cook for 5 to 7 minutes, or until meat is desired doneness, turning breasts over once or twice. Serve breasts and onion with sauce.

Per Serving: Calories: 200 • Protein: 20 g. • Carbohydrate: 13 g. • Fat: 7 g. • Cholesterol: 84 mg. • Sodium: 88 mg. Exchanges: 2¾ very lean meat, ½ vegetable, ¾ fruit, 1½ fat

Straw & Hay VERY FAST

"Straw and hay" is the translation for a northern Italian dish with green and white pasta. Use good-quality durum semolina fettucini and spinach fettucini for this dish.

2 tablespoons butter or margarine
4 boneless skinless wood duck breasts (3 to 4 oz. each), split in half, cut crosswise into ¼-inch strips
4 oz. uncooked white fettucini
4 oz. uncooked spinach fettucini

SAUCE:

2 tablespoons butter or margarine
2 cloves garlic, minced
¼ cup all-purpose flour
1 cup water
2 cups half-and-half
2½ teaspoons chicken bouillon granules
½ teaspoon ground nutmeg
1 cup frozen baby peas, defrosted (optional)

Shredded fresh Parmesan cheese (optional)

4 servings

In 10-inch skillet, melt 2 tablespoons butter over medium-high heat. Add duck strips. Cook for 2 to 3 minutes, or until meat is browned, stirring occasionally. Set aside and keep warm.

Prepare fettucini as directed on package. Drain. While fettucini is cooking, prepare sauce. In 2-quart saucepan, melt 2 tablespoons butter over medium heat. Add garlic. Cook for 30 seconds, stirring constantly. Stir in flour. Cook for 1 minute, stirring constantly. Gradually blend in water, stirring until smooth. Stir in half-and-half, bouillon and nutmeg. Cook for 4 to 5 minutes, or until sauce thickens and bubbles, stirring constantly. Stir in peas and duck. Cook for 1 to 2 minutes, or until heated through, stirring occasionally.

Spoon sauce over fettucini. Sprinkle with Parmesan cheese.

Per Serving: Calories: 632 • Protein: 32 g. • Carbohydrate: 53 g. • Fat: 31 g. • Cholesterol: 179 mg. • Sodium: 896 mg. Exchanges: 3½ starch, 2¾ very lean meat, 6¼ fat

Diving Ducks

Menu

Duck-Tortilla Torte (recipe below)

Tricolored Salad (recipe below) ❧ *Spanish Rice*

Duck-Tortilla Torte

1 jar (16 oz.) prepared green salsa, warmed
6 flour tortillas (7-inch), divided
2 cups (8 oz.) shredded cooked diving duck, divided
2 cups (8 oz.) shredded Colby-Jack cheese, divided
1 medium tomato, seeded and chopped

6 servings

Heat oven to 350°F. Place salsa in shallow dish. Dip 2 tortillas in warm salsa to coat. Arrange tortillas, slightly overlapping, in bottom of deep, 9-inch pie plate, tearing tortillas to fit. Spread 1 cup shredded duck over tortillas. Dip and layer 2 more tortillas. Sprinkle with 1 cup cheese.

Dip and layer remaining 2 tortillas. Spread remaining duck over tortillas. Pour remaining salsa over duck. Top evenly with remaining cheese, then the tomato.

Bake for 30 to 35 minutes, or until torte is heated through and cheese is melted and lightly browned. Let stand for 5 minutes. Serve torte in wedges garnished with sour cream, if desired.

Per Serving: Calories: 363 • Protein: 22 g.
• Carbohydrate: 22 g. • Fat: 19 g.
• Cholesterol: 75 mg. • Sodium: 921 mg.
Exchanges: 1 starch, 2½ very lean meat, 1¼ vegetable, 4 fat

Tricolored Salad

1 lb. fresh green beans, trimmed
1 small jícama root, peeled and cut into 3 × ¼-inch strips (2 cups)
2 red peppers, seeded and cut into ¼-inch strips

VINAIGRETTE:
½ cup olive oil
3 tablespoons fresh lime juice
2 tablespoons fresh lemon juice
1 clove garlic, minced
1 teaspoon chili powder
½ teaspoon dried oregano leaves
¼ teaspoon ground cumin
¼ teaspoon salt
¼ teaspoon pepper

Sliced black olives

6 servings

Bring large pot of water to a boil. Add beans to water. Cook for 4 to 5 minutes, or until beans are tender-crisp. Rinse beans under cold water to stop cooking. Drain well. Place beans, jícama and peppers in separate, shallow dishes. Set aside.

In small mixing bowl, combine vinaigrette ingredients. Whisk until smooth. Pour dressing evenly over vegetables. Stir to coat. Cover each dish with plastic wrap. Chill 1 hour, stirring vegetables once or twice.

To serve, arrange vegetables on lettuce-lined serving platter. Drizzle any remaining dressing from dishes over vegetables. Garnish with olives.

Per Serving: Calories: 209 • Protein: 2 g. • Carbohydrate: 11 g. • Fat: 18 g.
• Cholesterol: 0 mg. • Sodium: 102 mg.
Exchanges: 2¼ vegetable, 3½ fat

Duck Cassoulet

6 oz. spicy sausage, sliced
8 oz. boneless skinless diving
   duck meat, cut into ½-inch
   cubes
1 medium yellow squash, sliced
   (1 cup)
1 cup chopped leek
1 medium carrot, sliced
   (½ cup)
2 cloves garlic, minced
1 can (15½ oz.) Great Northern
   beans, rinsed and drained
1 can (15½ oz.) pinto beans,
   rinsed and drained
1 can (14½ oz.) Italian-seasoned
   diced tomatoes, undrained
1 teaspoon dried thyme leaves
⅓ cup unseasoned dried bread
   crumbs
2 tablespoons butter, melted

4 to 6 servings

Heat oven to 350°F. In 4-quart saucepan, cook sausage and duck cubes over medium heat for 8 to 10 minutes, or until meat is browned, stirring occasionally. Using slotted spoon, remove meat from skillet. Set aside.

To drippings in skillet, add squash, leek, carrot and garlic. Cook over medium heat for 4 to 6 minutes, or until vegetables are tender-crisp, stirring occasionally. Remove from heat. Stir in meat and remaining ingredients, except crumbs and butter. Spoon mixture into 2-quart casserole.

Bake cassoulet for 25 to 30 minutes, or until bubbly around edges. Remove from oven. In small bowl, combine crumbs and butter. Sprinkle mixture evenly over cassoulet. Place under broiler with surface of cassoulet 4 to 5 inches from heat. Broil for 2 to 3 minutes, or until crumbs are lightly browned.

Per Serving: Calories: 342 • Protein: 18 g.
• Carbohydrate: 25 g. • Fat: 19 g.
• Cholesterol: 59 mg. • Sodium: 659 mg.
Exchanges: 1½ starch, 2 medium-fat meat,
½ vegetable, 1½ fat

Calvados Duck →

Calvados is a dry apple brandy made in the Normandy region of France. It is often used for cooking poultry. Applejack is its American cousin.

¾ cup Calvados or applejack
¾ cup vegetable oil
2 whole dressed diving ducks
    (1 to 1¼ lbs. each), skin
    removed, quartered
3 sprigs fresh rosemary
1 tablespoon juniper berries,
    crushed

4 servings

In 2-cup measure, combine Calvados and oil. Whisk to blend. Arrange duck halves in 13 × 9-inch baking dish. Pour Calvados mixture over ducks, turning to coat. Place rosemary and juniper berries in dish around ducks. Cover with plastic wrap. Refrigerate overnight, turning ducks occasionally.

Prepare grill for medium direct heat. Spray cooking grid with nonstick vegetable cooking spray. Drain and discard marinade from ducks. Grill ducks for 15 to 18 minutes, or until meat is desired doneness, turning duck halves occasionally.

Per Serving: Calories: 249 • Protein: 23 g.
• Carbohydrate: 4 g. • Fat: 15 g.
• Cholesterol: 88 mg. • Sodium: 66 mg.
Exchanges: 3¼ lean meat, 1 fat

Curry Glazed Ducks

¼ cup butter or margarine
½ cup apricot preserves
1 teaspoon curry powder
2 whole dressed diving ducks
    (1 to 1¼ lbs. each), skin
    removed, quartered

4 servings

In 1-quart saucepan, melt butter over medium heat. Stir in preserves and curry powder. Cook for 1 minute, stirring constantly. Remove glaze from heat.

Prepare grill for medium direct heat. Spray cooking grid with nonstick vegetable cooking spray. Grill duck pieces, uncovered, for 24 minutes, turning once. Brush duck with glaze. Grill for 5 to 10 minutes longer, or until meat is desired doneness, turning pieces and brushing with glaze occasionally.

Per Serving: Calories: 341 • Protein: 23 g. • Carbohydrate: 26 g. • Fat: 17 g.
• Cholesterol: 119 mg. • Sodium: 199 mg.
Exchanges: 3¼ lean meat, 1¼ fat

Lemon & Rosemary Duck Breasts ⟨LOW-FAT↑⟩

MARINADE:

1/3 cup olive oil
1 teaspoon grated lemon peel
2 tablespoons fresh lemon juice
2 tablespoons snipped fresh rosemary, or
   2 teaspoons dried rosemary leaves
   Coarsely ground pepper to taste

2 whole boneless skinless diving duck breasts
   (8 to 10 oz. each), split in half
1/4 teaspoon salt

4 servings

In shallow dish, combine marinade ingredients. Add duck breast halves, turning to coat. Cover with plastic wrap. Refrigerate at least 4 hours, turning breast halves occasionally.

Prepare grill for medium direct heat. Spray cooking grid with nonstick vegetable cooking spray. Drain and discard marinade from breast halves. Sprinkle evenly with salt. Grill, covered, for 10 to 15 minutes, or until meat is desired doneness, turning breast halves occasionally.

Per Serving: Calories: 196 • Protein: 25 g. • Carbohydrate: <1 g. • Fat: 10 g. • Cholesterol: 98 mg. • Sodium: 208 mg. Exchanges: 3½ very lean meat, 2 fat

Duck with Honey-Chili Glaze ⟨LOW-FAT⟩

3/4 cup honey
1/2 cup prepared chili sauce
1/4 cup frozen orange juice concentrate, defrosted
1 to 2 teaspoons grated orange peel
2 whole dressed diving ducks (1 to 1¼ lbs. each),
   skin removed, split in half
   Fresh orange slices

4 servings

Heat oven to 350°F. In 2-cup measure, combine honey, chili sauce, concentrate and peel. Reserve 3/4 cup sauce.

Spray 13 × 9-inch baking dish with nonstick vegetable cooking spray. Arrange duck halves in baking dish. Pour remaining sauce over ducks. Cover with foil. Bake for 30 minutes. Remove foil. Bake 30 to 35 minutes longer, or until meat is desired doneness, basting frequently with juices in dish.

In 1-quart saucepan, warm reserved sauce over medium heat. Serve duck with warm sauce. Garnish with orange slices.

Per Serving: Calories: 401 • Protein: 24 g. • Carbohydrate: 68 g. • Fat: 5 g. • Cholesterol: 88 mg. • Sodium: 525 mg. Exchanges: 3¼ very lean meat, 1 vegetable, ½ fruit, 1 fat

Creole Duck

½ cup butter or margarine, divided
1 medium green pepper, seeded and chopped (1¼ cups)
1 medium onion, chopped (1 cup)
8 oz. fresh mushrooms, sliced (3 cups)
2 cloves garlic, minced
2 cans (14½ oz. each) diced tomatoes
1 cup ready-to-serve chicken broth
2 bay leaves
1½ teaspoons chili powder
1 teaspoon ground cumin
½ teaspoon dried thyme leaves
¼ teaspoon ground allspice
¼ teaspoon red pepper flakes
2 whole dressed diving ducks (1 to 1¼ lbs. each), skin removed, quartered
4 cups hot cooked white rice

4 servings

In 2-quart saucepan, melt ¼ cup butter over medium heat. Add pepper and onion. Cook for 3 to 4 minutes, or until vegetables are tender-crisp, stirring occasionally. Stir in mushrooms and garlic. Cook for 1 to 2 minutes, or until vegetables are tender, stirring occasionally.

Stir in remaining ingredients, except ducks and rice. Bring to a boil over high heat. Reduce heat to low. Simmer for 10 to 15 minutes, or until sauce is thickened. Remove and discard bay leaves.

Meanwhile, in 6-quart Dutch oven, melt remaining ¼ cup butter over medium heat. Add duck pieces. Cook for 3 to 4 minutes, or until browned, turning pieces occasionally. Pour sauce over duck pieces. Bring to a boil. Cover. Reduce heat to medium-low. Simmer for 30 to 40 minutes, or until meat is tender. Serve mixture over rice.

Per Serving: Calories: 705 • Protein: 33 g. • Carbohydrate: 76 g. • Fat: 30 g.
• Cholesterol: 150 mg. • Sodium: 903 mg.
Exchanges: 3½ starch, 3¼ lean meat, 4 vegetable, 4 fat

Duck Diane VERY FAST ↓

SAUCE:
1 tablespoon lemon juice
1 tablespoon Worcestershire sauce
1 tablespoon snipped fresh chives
1 teaspoon brandy

½ teaspoon dry mustard
1 whole boneless skinless diving duck breast
    (8 to 10 oz.), split in half, pounded to
    ¼-inch thickness
2 tablespoons butter

2 servings

In small bowl, combine sauce ingredients. Set aside. Sprinkle mustard evenly over duck breast halves.

In 10-inch skillet, melt butter over medium heat. Add breast halves. Cook for 8 to 10 minutes, or until meat is desired doneness, turning breast halves over once or twice. Pour sauce over duck. Cook for 30 seconds longer to warm sauce. Serve duck with pan drippings drizzled over top.

Per Serving: Calories: 247 • Protein: 26 g. • Carbohydrate: 6 g. • Fat: 12 g. • Cholesterol: 165 mg. • Sodium: 335 mg.
Exchanges: 3½ very lean meat, 2½ fat

Blackened Duck VERY FAST

SPICE MIX:
2 teaspoons sweet paprika
½ to 1 teaspoon salt
½ teaspoon garlic powder
½ teaspoon onion powder
½ teaspoon cayenne
¼ teaspoon white pepper
¼ teaspoon black pepper
¼ teaspoon dried thyme leaves
¼ teaspoon dried oregano leaves

¼ cup butter, melted
2 whole boneless skinless diving duck breasts
    (8 to 10 oz. each), split in half

4 servings

In shallow dish, combine spice mix ingredients. Place butter in second shallow dish. Dip duck breast halves in butter, then dredge in spice mix to coat.

Heat 12-inch nonstick skillet over medium-high heat. Add breast halves. Drizzle with remaining butter. Cook for 8 to 10 minutes, or until meat is desired doneness, turning breast halves once or twice.

Per Serving: Calories: 266 • Protein: 26 g. • Carbohydrate: 1 g. • Fat: 17 g. • Cholesterol: 129 mg. • Sodium: 602 mg.
Exchanges: 3½ very lean meat, 3¼ fat

Grilled Duck with Pepper Jelly Glaze

1 tablespoon kosher salt
1 teaspoon pepper
½ teaspoon dried thyme leaves
½ teaspoon dried rosemary leaves
2 whole boneless skinless diving duck breasts (8 to 10 oz. each), split in half
2 cups ready-to-serve chicken broth
½ cup raspberry white wine vinegar
2 tablespoons chopped shallots
2 tablespoons pepper jelly
3 tablespoons butter, chopped

4 servings

In small bowl, combine salt, pepper, thyme and rosemary. Sprinkle duck breast halves evenly with herb mixture. Cover with plastic wrap. Refrigerate at least 4 hours.

In 1-quart saucepan, combine broth, vinegar and shallots. Bring to a boil over high heat. Reduce heat to medium. Simmer for 20 to 25 minutes, or until reduced to 1 cup. Stir in jelly. Bring to a boil over high heat. Reduce heat to medium. Simmer for 8 to 10 minutes, or until reduced to ½ cup. Add butter. Whisk until blended. Set glaze aside and keep warm.

Prepare grill for medium direct heat. Spray cooking grid with nonstick vegetable cooking spray. Grill breast halves, covered, for 10 to 14 minutes, or until browned. Turn breast halves. Grill for 3 to 5 minutes longer, or until meat is desired doneness.

Slice each breast half crosswise into 5 or 6 strips. Fan strips on individual serving plates. Spoon glaze evenly over each.

Per Serving: Calories: 283 • Protein: 27 g. • Carbohydrate: 8 g. • Fat: 15 g.
• Cholesterol: 121 mg. • Sodium: 1768 mg.
Exchanges: 3¾ lean meat, ¼ vegetable, ¾ fat

Duck Mole

Mole (MO-lay) is a rich, spicy Mexican sauce usually served with poultry.

SAUCE:

- 8 oz. fresh Roma tomatoes, sliced
- 1 fresh Anaheim chili, cut lengthwise into quarters and seeded
- 1 corn tortilla (6-inch)
- 4½ teaspoons sesame seed
- 3 tablespoons vegetable oil, divided
- 1 small onion, chopped (½ cup)
- 3 cloves garlic, minced
- 1 can (11 oz.) tomatillos
- 2 dried New Mexico red chilies, crumbled
- 1 tablespoon raisins
- 2 cups ready-to-serve chicken broth
- 1 can (4 oz.) chopped green chilies
- 3 tablespoons semisweet chocolate chips
- ¼ to ½ teaspoon salt
- ¼ teaspoon dried oregano leaves
- ¼ teaspoon ground cinnamon
- ¼ teaspoon ground allspice
- ⅛ teaspoon dried thyme leaves

- 2 whole dressed diving ducks (1 to 1¼ lbs. each), skin removed, split in half
- 4 cups hot cooked white rice
  Fresh cilantro leaves

4 servings

Spray baking sheet with nonstick vegetable cooking spray. Arrange tomato slices and Anaheim chili on baking sheet. Place under broiler with surface of vegetables 4 to 5 inches from heat. Broil for 4 to 5 minutes, or until vegetables are blackened, turning vegetables occasionally. Set aside.

Heat oven to 350°F. Place tortilla and sesame seed on baking sheet with edges. Bake for 3 to 4 minutes, or until tortilla is crisp and sesame seed is lightly browned. Break tortilla into pieces. Set aside.

In 10-inch skillet, heat 1 tablespoon oil over medium-high heat. Add onion and garlic. Cook for 4 to 6 minutes, or until vegetables are tender, stirring frequently. Stir in tomatillos, dried chilies and raisins. Cook for 1 minute, stirring constantly. Remove from heat.

In food processor or blender, combine tomatillo mixture, broiled tomatoes and Anaheim chili, tortilla, sesame seed, broth and green chilies. Process until smooth. Pour mixture into 3-quart saucepan. Cook over medium heat for 10 to 15 minutes, or until sauce thickens and becomes darker. Stir in remaining sauce ingredients. Reduce heat to medium-low. Simmer for 40 minutes to blend flavors, stirring occasionally. Set sauce aside.

Heat oven to 350°F. In 12-inch nonstick skillet, heat 1 tablespoon oil over medium-high heat. Add 2 duck halves. Cook for 6 to 8 minutes, or until browned, turning duck halves occasionally. Place duck halves in 13 × 9-inch baking dish. Repeat with remaining 1 tablespoon oil and 2 duck halves.

Pour mole sauce evenly over duck. Bake for 1 to 1¼ hours, or until meat is tender, turning duck once or twice. Serve duck mole over rice. Garnish with cilantro leaves.

TIP: Mole sauce can be made up to 2 days ahead and refrigerated in an airtight container.

Per Serving: Calories: 650 • Protein: 32 g. • Carbohydrate: 81 g. • Fat: 21 g.
• Cholesterol: 88 mg. • Sodium: 1063 mg.
Exchanges: 3½ starch, 3 lean meat, 1 vegetable, 2¼ fat

Gumbo

Make this recipe when you're having a big group over.

½ cup vegetable oil

½ cup all-purpose flour

11 cups water, divided

3 green peppers, seeded and chopped (3½ cups)

2 medium onions, chopped (2 cups)

4 stalks celery, sliced (2 cups)

1 red pepper, seeded and chopped (1¼ cups)

2 pkgs. (10 oz. each) frozen sliced okra

1 smoked turkey sausage (16 oz.), cut into ½-inch slices

3 tablespoons chicken bouillon granules

1½ tablespoons salt

1 tablespoon red pepper sauce

2 teaspoons cayenne

2 teaspoons black pepper

2 bay leaves

1 teaspoon white pepper

½ teaspoon garlic powder

½ teaspoon Creole seasoning

8 oz. boneless skinless diving duck meat, cut into ¾-inch cubes

2 tablespoons filé powder*

12 to 14 cups hot cooked white rice
    Snipped fresh parsley (optional)
    Sliced green onions (optional)

12 to 14 servings

In 8-quart stockpot, heat oil over medium-high heat. Stir in flour. Cook for 12 to 15 minutes, or until mixture is a deep golden brown, stirring constantly. Whisk in 1 cup water.

Add green peppers, onions, celery and red pepper. Reduce heat to medium. Cook for 5 to 7 minutes, or until vegetables are tender-crisp. Stir in remaining 10 cups water and remaining ingredients, except duck, filé powder, rice, parsley and green onions. Bring to a boil over medium-high heat. Reduce heat to medium-low. Simmer gumbo for 40 minutes to blend flavors. Remove and discard bay leaves.

Meanwhile, heat 10-inch nonstick skillet over medium heat. Spray skillet with nonstick vegetable cooking spray. Add duck meat. Cook for 3 to 5 minutes, or until meat is no longer pink, stirring occasionally. Add meat to gumbo. Cook for 15 to 20 minutes longer, or until meat is tender. Stir in filé powder.

Serve gumbo over rice. Garnish with parsley and green onions.

*Filé powder is made from the ground, dried leaves of the sassafras tree. It is a common ingredient in Creole cooking and is used to flavor and thicken gumbo.

Per Serving: Calories: 464 • Protein: 16 g. • Carbohydrate: 72 g. • Fat: 12 g. • Cholesterol: 30 mg. • Sodium: 1919 mg.
Exchanges: 3½ starch, 1 lean meat, 1½ vegetable, 1½ fat

Hunan Duck ⬩LOW-FAT⬩

MARINADE:
- ½ cup apricot preserves
- ½ cup hoisin sauce
- ¼ cup soy sauce
- ¼ cup molasses
- 3 tablespoons packed brown sugar
- 2 tablespoons chopped crystallized gingerroot
- 2 teaspoons chili paste
- 2 cloves garlic, minced

- 2 whole boneless skinless diving duck breasts (8 to 10 oz. each), split in half

4 servings

In 2-cup measure, combine marinade ingredients. Arrange duck breast halves in 13 × 9-inch baking dish. Pour marinade over breast halves, turning to coat. Cover with plastic wrap. Refrigerate 24 hours, turning breast halves occasionally.

Prepare grill for medium direct heat. Spray cooking grid with nonstick vegetable cooking spray. Arrange breast halves skin-side-down on cooking grid. Grill, covered, for 10 to 15 minutes, or until meat is desired doneness, turning breast halves once or twice.

Per Serving: Calories: 318 • Protein: 26 g. • Carbohydrate: 39 g. • Fat: 5 g. • Cholesterol: 98 mg. • Sodium: 974 mg.
Exchanges: 3½ very lean meat, 1 fat

Duck Mulligatawny ⬩LOW-FAT⬩ ↓

Mulligatawny soup is a curry-flavored dish from southern India. Its name means "pepper water." Preparing it in the slow cooker makes this an ideal recipe for older, tougher birds.

- 2 tablespoons butter or margarine
- 1 lb. boneless skinless diving duck meat, cut into ¾-inch cubes
- 1 medium onion, chopped (1 cup)
- 2 stalks celery, sliced (1 cup)
- 2 tablespoons all-purpose flour
- 2 cloves garlic, minced
- 1 tablespoon curry powder
- ½ teaspoon ground coriander
- ½ teaspoon ground cumin
- ¼ teaspoon white pepper (optional)
- 6 cups hot water or chicken broth
- 2 tart, red cooking apples, cored and chopped (2 cups)
- ⅔ cup tomato juice

6 servings

In 12-inch nonstick skillet, melt butter over medium heat. Add duck meat. Cook for 3 to 4 minutes, or until meat is no longer pink, stirring occasionally. Stir in onion, celery, flour, garlic, curry powder, coriander, cumin and pepper. Cook for 3 minutes, stirring constantly.

Place duck mixture in 4-quart slow cooker. Add water, apples and tomato juice. Cook on low for 8 to 10 hours, or until meat is tender, stirring occasionally. Serve soup over rice, garnished with snipped fresh parsley and raw coconut shavings, if desired.

Per Serving: Calories: 188 • Protein: 15 g. • Carbohydrate: 13 g. • Fat: 9 g. • Cholesterol: 69 mg. • Sodium: 213 mg.
Exchanges: ¼ starch, 2 lean meat, ¾ vegetable, ¼ fruit, ½ fat

Jambalaya

- 3 strips bacon, chopped
- 1 smoked turkey sausage (16 oz.), cut into ½-inch slices
- 8 oz. boneless skinless diving duck meat, cut into ½-inch cubes
- 1 green pepper, seeded and chopped (1¼ cups)
- 1 medium onion, chopped (1 cup)
- 3 cloves garlic, minced
- 1 can (14½ oz.) diced tomatoes
- 1 cup ready-to-serve chicken broth
- 1 cup tomato juice
- 1 bay leaf
- 1 to 2 teaspoons red pepper sauce
- ½ to 1 teaspoon cayenne
- ½ teaspoon salt
- ½ teaspoon black pepper
- ½ teaspoon Creole seasoning
- ¼ to ½ teaspoon red pepper flakes
- 1 cup uncooked white rice
- 1 lb. fresh medium shrimp, shelled and deveined
  Snipped fresh parsley

8 servings

In 6-quart Dutch oven or stockpot, cook bacon over medium heat for 3 to 4 minutes, or until edges begin to crisp, stirring occasionally. Stir in sausage, duck meat, green pepper, onion and garlic. Increase heat to medium-high. Cook for 5 to 6 minutes, or until meat is no longer pink.

Stir in tomatoes, broth, juice, bay leaf, red pepper sauce, cayenne, salt, black pepper, Creole seasoning and red pepper flakes. Bring to a boil. Cover. Reduce heat to medium-low. Simmer for 10 minutes. Stir in rice. Re-cover. Simmer for 15 minutes longer. Stir in shrimp. Re-cover. Reduce heat to low. Simmer for 20 to 30 minutes, or until rice is tender, stirring once or twice. Remove and discard bay leaf. Garnish jambalaya with parsley.

Per Serving: Calories: 333 • Protein: 27 g.
• Carbohydrate: 28 g. • Fat: 12 g.
• Cholesterol: 127 mg. • Sodium: 1472 mg.
Exchanges: 1¼ starch, 3 lean meat,
1½ vegetable, ¾ fat

Tiny Ducks

Menu

Raspberry-glazed Ducks (recipe below)

Orange Pecan Rice (recipe below)

Snap Pea Sauté (recipe below) ❧ *Dinner Rolls*

Raspberry-glazed Ducks FAST

¹/₂ cup raspberry jam	4 whole dressed teals
2 tablespoons raspberry-flavored vinegar	(8 oz. each)
2 tablespoons orange-flavored liqueur	Fresh raspberries

4 servings

Heat oven to 425°F. In 1-quart saucepan, combine jam, vinegar and liqueur. Bring to a boil over medium-high heat. Reserve ¹/₃ cup sauce. Set remaining sauce aside and keep warm.

Spray rack in roasting pan with nonstick vegetable cooking spray. Arrange ducks breast-side-up on rack. Roast for 20 minutes. Brush ducks evenly with reserved ¹/₃ cup sauce. Roast for 5 to 10 minutes longer, or until meat is tender and juices run clear. Garnish ducks with fresh raspberries and serve with remaining sauce.

Per Serving: Calories: 406 • Protein: 24 g. • Carbohydrate: 28 g. • Fat: 21 g. • Cholesterol: 109 mg. • Sodium: 92 mg.
Exchanges: 3¹/₂ medium-fat meat, ¹/₂ fat

Orange Pecan Rice FAST

1 can (14¹/₂ oz.) ready-to-serve chicken broth	¹/₂ cup coarsely chopped pecans
2 tablespoons cream sherry	¹/₄ cup sliced green onions
2 tablespoons fresh orange juice	2 tablespoons grated orange peel
1 cup uncooked long-grain white rice	1 tablespoon butter or margarine
	1 clove garlic, minced

4 servings

In 2-cup measure, combine broth, sherry, juice and enough water to make 2 cups liquid. Pour liquid into 2-quart saucepan. Bring to a boil over high heat. Stir in rice. Cover. Reduce heat to medium-low. Simmer for 15 to 20 minutes, or until rice is tender and liquid is absorbed.

Stir in pecans, onions, peel, butter and garlic. Cook for 1 to 2 minutes, or until butter melts and mixture is heated through, stirring frequently.

Per Serving: Calories: 319 • Protein: 5 g. • Carbohydrate: 43 g. • Fat: 13 g. • Cholesterol: 8 mg. • Sodium: 471 mg.
Exchanges: 2¹/₄ starch, 2¹/₂ fat

Snap Pea Sauté FAST

2 tablespoons butter or margarine
1 tablespoon finely chopped onion
2 cups fresh or frozen sugar snap peas
2 tablespoons water
¹/₄ teaspoon salt
¹/₈ teaspoon white pepper
2 tablespoons snipped fresh parsley

4 servings

In 12-inch skillet, melt butter over medium-high heat. Add onion. Cook for 1 to 2 minutes, or until onion is tender, stirring frequently. Stir in remaining ingredients, except parsley. Cover. Cook for 3 to 4 minutes, or until peas are tender-crisp, stirring occasionally. Sprinkle with parsley just before serving.

Per Serving: Calories: 79 • Protein: 2 g. • Carbohydrate: 5 g. • Fat: 6 g. • Cholesterol: 16 mg. • Sodium: 194 mg.
Exchanges: 1 vegetable, 1 fat

Orange Duck Salad with Toasted Almonds ⬤ VERY FAST ↓

4 cups mixed salad greens
1 medium orange, peeled and sectioned, membranes removed
1 small red onion, sliced
½ cup slivered almonds, toasted
4 whole boneless skinless teal breasts (3 to 4 oz. each)
¼ cup vegetable oil
2 tablespoons orange juice
1 tablespoon olive oil
1 tablespoon Dijon mustard
  Freshly ground pepper to taste

4 servings

Arrange salad greens evenly on individual serving plates. Arrange orange, onion and almonds evenly over greens. Set aside.

Prepare grill for medium direct heat. Spray cooking grid with nonstick vegetable cooking spray. Grill duck breasts for 12 to 15 minutes, or until meat is desired doneness, turning breasts over once or twice Cut breasts into strips. Arrange strips evenly on serv ing plates.

In 1-cup measure, combine remaining ingredients, except pepper. Whisk until blended. Drizzle evenly over salads. Sprinkle salads with pepper.

Per Serving: Calories: 388 • Protein: 24 g. • Carbohydrate: 12 g. • Fat: 28 g. • Cholesterol: 76 mg. • Sodium: 166 mg.
Exchanges: 2¾ very lean meat, 2 vegetable, 5½ fat

Teal Eggroll Triangles

1 cup (4 oz.) chopped uncooked teal meat
1 cup chopped fresh mushrooms
1½ teaspoons salt, divided
1 teaspoon cornstarch
½ teaspoon soy sauce
4 cups water
8 cups shredded green cabbage
1 tablespoon sesame oil
½ cup sliced green onions
1 teaspoon five-spice powder
8 eggroll skins (7-inch square)
1¼ cups vegetable oil
  Sweet and sour sauce (optional)
  Hot mustard (optional)

4 servings

In small mixing bowl, combine duck meat, mushrooms, ½ teaspoon salt, the cornstarch and soy sauce. Mix well. Cover with plastic wrap. Refrigerate 30 minutes, stirring occasionally.

In 3-quart saucepan, bring water to a boil over high heat. Add cabbage. Cook for 3 to 4 minutes, or until cabbage is tender-crisp. Rinse cabbage under cold water until cool. Drain well, squeezing cabbage to remove excess moisture. Place cabbage in large mixing bowl. Set aside.

In 12-inch skillet, heat sesame oil over medium-high heat. Add duck mixture. Cook for 3 to 5 minutes, or until meat is no longer pink, stirring frequently. Add duck mixture, onions, five-spice powder and remaining 1 teaspoon salt to cabbage. Stir to combine.

Spoon cabbage mixture evenly onto centers of eggroll skins (about ½ cup each). Brush edges of eggroll skins lightly with water. Fold eggroll skins in half, matching opposite corners to form triangles. Press edges to seal. Cover triangles with plastic wrap.

In 12-inch skillet, heat vegetable oil over medium-high heat. Add 2 eggroll triangles to skillet. Cook for 2 to 4 minutes, or until golden brown, turning triangles over once. Drain on paper-towel-lined plate and keep warm. Repeat with remaining triangles. Serve with sweet and sour sauce and hot mustard.

Per Serving: Calories: 359 • Protein: 14 g. • Carbohydrate: 47 g. • Fat: 13 g. • Cholesterol: 28 mg. • Sodium: 1277 mg.
Exchanges: 2¼ starch, ¾ very lean meat, 2½ vegetable, 2½ fat

Duck Wellington

5 tablespoons butter or margarine, divided
1 small onion, finely chopped (1/2 cup)
8 oz. fresh mushrooms, finely chopped (2 1/2 cups)
1 tablespoon Dijon mustard
1/2 teaspoon dried thyme leaves
4 whole boneless skinless teal breasts
    (3 to 4 oz. each), split in half
3 tablespoons all-purpose flour
1 cup ready-to-serve chicken broth
2 tablespoons dry sherry
1 pkg. (17 oz.) frozen puff pastry sheets, defrosted
1 egg, beaten with 2 teaspoons water

4 servings

In 12-inch skillet, melt 2 tablespoons butter over medium heat. Add onion. Cook for 2 to 3 minutes, or until onion is tender, stirring occasionally. Stir in mushrooms. Cook for 3 to 4 minutes, or until mushrooms weep and liquid is evaporated, stirring occasionally. Stir in mustard and thyme. Set filling aside.

In 10-inch skillet, melt remaining 3 tablespoons butter over medium heat. Add duck breast halves. Cook for 5 to 7 minutes, or until meat is desired doneness, turning breast halves once or twice. Remove duck breasts from skillet. Set aside.

Stir flour into drippings in skillet. Cook over medium heat for 2 minutes, stirring constantly. Blend in broth and sherry. Bring to a boil. Boil sauce for 1 minute, stirring constantly. Stir 3 tablespoons sauce into mushroom mixture. Cover remaining sauce with plastic wrap and refrigerate.

Spray baking sheet with nonstick vegetable cooking spray. Set aside. On lightly floured surface, roll pastry sheets into 10-inch squares. Cut each sheet in half. Spoon mushroom mixture evenly onto center of each piece of pastry (about 1/3 cup each). Top each piece with 2 duck breast halves. Fold pastry over duck, overlapping only enough to seal. (Trim excess pastry, if necessary.) Moisten edges of pastry with water, pinching to seal. Place pastry packets seam-side-down on prepared baking sheet. Cover with plastic wrap. Refrigerate 1 hour.

Heat oven to 400°F. Brush pastry packets lightly with egg mixture. Pierce tops of packets several times with wooden pick. Bake for 25 to 30 minutes, or until packets are golden brown. Meanwhile, warm remaining sauce over medium-low heat until hot. Serve sauce with pastry packets.

Per Serving: Calories: 1014 • Protein: 33 g. • Carbohydrate: 66 g.
• Fat: 67 g. • Cholesterol: 168 mg. • Sodium: 867 mg.
Exchanges: 3 3/4 starch, 3 very lean meat, 2 vegetable, 13 1/2 fat

Duck & Vegetable Sauté ↓

8 oz. uncooked linguine
1 tablespoon olive oil
4 whole boneless skinless teal breasts
    (3 to 4 oz. each), split in half
6 oz. fresh mushrooms, sliced (2 cups)
2 medium zucchini, sliced (2 cups)
2 cloves garlic, minced
1 medium tomato, seeded and chopped
1 can (4 oz.) chopped green chilies, drained
1/2 teaspoon salt
1/4 teaspoon pepper
1/2 cup shredded fresh Parmesan cheese

4 servings

Prepare linguine as directed on package. Drain. Meanwhile, in 12-inch nonstick skillet, heat oil over medium-high heat. Add duck breast halves, mushrooms, zucchini and garlic. Cook for 5 to 7 minutes, or until meat is no longer pink, stirring occasionally.

Stir in tomato, chilies, salt and pepper. Cook for 2 to 3 minutes, or until heated through, stirring occasionally. Spoon mixture over prepared linguine. Sprinkle with Parmesan cheese.

Per Serving: Calories: 444 • Protein: 33 g. • Carbohydrate: 50 g.
• Fat: 12 g. • Cholesterol: 84 mg. • Sodium: 670 mg.
Exchanges: 2 3/4 starch, 3 1/4 very lean meat,
1 3/4 vegetable,
2 1/4 fat

Index

A

Accompaniments and Side Dishes,
Broiled Vegetable Mélange, 71
Cranberry-Apple Chutney, 58
Cranberry Corn Bread Dressing, 11
Cucumber-Yogurt Salad, 44
Garlic Mashed Potatoes, 14
Herbed Focaccia, 31
Orange Pecan Rice, 120
Potato Galette with Chive Sour Cream, 95
Pumpkin Soup, 11
Snap Pea Sauté, 120
Tricolored Salad, 108
Winter Fruit Dressing, 80
Appetizers,
Cajun Pheasant Fingers, 22
Danish-pickled Spruce Grouse, 55
Dijon Pheasant Legs, 22
Goose Jerky, 85
Smoked Goose, 84
Teal Eggroll Triangles, 122
Woodcock Pâté, 77
Woodcock Rumaki, 76
Apple-Apricot Quail Couscous, 67
Apple Cider Partridge, 39
Apple-Ginger Ruffed Grouse, 32
Apples,
Apple-Apricot Quail Couscous, 67
Apple Cider Partridge, 39
Apple-Ginger Ruffed Grouse, 32
Chutney-Ginger Sharptail, 46
Cranberry-Apple Chutney, 58
Duck Mulligatawny, 118
Fruit-braised Goose Breast, 83
Horseradish Prairie Chicken, 52
Smoked Duck Hash Packets, 104
Winter Fruit Dressing, 80
Wood Duck with Apples & Apricots, 106
Apricot-glazed Goose, 83
Apricots,
Apple-Apricot Quail Couscous, 67
Apricot-glazed Goose, 83
Curry Glazed Ducks, 111
Fruit-braised Goose Breast, 83
Quail with Apricot Dressing, 68
Sage Grouse with Figs & Apricots, 55
Winter Fruit Dressing, 80
Wood Duck with Apples & Apricots, 106
Artichoke & Parmesan Stuffed Partridge
Rolls, 51

B

Baked Dishes,
Artichoke & Parmesan Stuffed Partridge
Rolls, 51
Blue Grouse Madeira with Chutney, 36
Cherry-sauced Quail, 63
Chukar Partridge in Rosemary-Cream
Sauce, 39
Cranberry-Jalapeño Glazed Duck Breast, 98
Creamy Ruffed Grouse with Rosemary, 34

Dijon Pheasant Legs, 22
Doves in Bread Dressing, 75
Duck with Honey-Chili Glaze, 112
Easy Pheasant Pie, 26
Fennel-braised Blue Grouse, 37
Five-spice Prairie Chicken, 54
Grape Leaf Wrapped Quail, 63
Hungarian Partridge Hunter's Style, 48
Hungarian Partridge with Juniper, 48
Lemon-Rosemary Chukar Partridge, 37
Mediterranean Pheasant with Onions, 20
Minted Blue Grouse, 36
Pecan Turkey with Maple Sauce, 12
Quail en Papillote, 65
Quail with Apricot Dressing, 68
Sage Grouse with Figs & Apricots, 55
Sherry-Cream Pheasant, 21
Smoked Duck Hash Packets, 104
Sun-dried Tomato Duck Breasts, 102
White Pheasant Pizza with Roasted
Red Pepper, 27
Barbecued Goose Sandwiches, 91
Barbecue-smoked Turkey, 12
Billy's Spicy Oriental Sharptail, 44
Blackberry-Duck Salad, 106
Blackened Duck, 114
Blue Grouse Madeira with Chutney, 36
Broiled Dishes,
Broiled Quail, 58
Broiled Vegetable Mélange, 71
Dove Breasts in Creamy Pepper Sauce, 71
Horseradish-Ginger Duck Breasts, 99
Peach-sauced Quail, 68
Rosemary-Garlic Quail with Baby Squash, 66
Broiled Quail, 58
Broiled Vegetable Mélange, 71

C

Cajun Pheasant Fingers, 22
Calvados Duck, 111
Casseroles,
Duck Cassoulet, 110
Goose Lasagna Casserole, 93
Risotto Grouse Casserole, 42
Spanish Rice & Goose Casserole, 93
Zesty Goose & Rice Casserole, 88
Cherry-sauced Quail, 63
Chestnuts & Cranberries, Ruffed Grouse
with, 35
Chicken-fried Pheasant, 14
Chilies/Chili Peppers,
Cranberry-Jalapeño Glazed Duck Breast, 98
Duck & Vegetable Sauté, 123
Duck Mole, 116
Preparing or roasting chili peppers, 38, 53
Sweet & Hot Glazed Chukars, 38
Chowder, see: Soups and Chowders
Chukar Partridge in Rosemary-Cream
Sauce, 39
Chukar Partridge with Lentils, 43
Chukar Partridge with Pears, 31
Chutney,
Blue Grouse Madeira with Chutney, 36
Cranberry-Apple Chutney, 58
Chutney-Ginger Sharptail, 46
Chutney-Ginger Sharptail, 46
Couscous,
Apple-Apricot Quail Couscous, 67
Moroccan Goose Couscous, 91
Moroccan Grilled Sharptail, 47

Cranberries,
Chutney-Ginger Sharptail, 46
Cranberry-Apple Chutney, 58
Cranberry Corn Bread Dressing, 11
Cranberry-glazed Pheasant, 17
Cranberry-Jalapeño Glazed Duck Breast, 98
Cranberry-Pheasant Wild Rice Salad, 28
Fruity Garlic-roasted Pheasant, 19
Ruffed Grouse with Chestnuts &
Cranberries, 35
Winter Fruit Dressing, 80
Cranberry-Apple Chutney, 58
Cranberry Corn Bread Dressing, 11
Cranberry-glazed Pheasant, 17
Cranberry-Jalapeño Glazed Duck Breast, 98
Cranberry-Pheasant Wild Rice Salad, 28
Creamed Pheasant & Biscuits, 19
Creamy Ruffed Grouse with Rosemary, 34
Creamy Wild Rice-Duck Soup, 103
Creole Duck, 113
Cucumber-Yogurt Salad, 44
Currant-Mustard Goose Breast, 85
Curried Goose & Spinach, 89
Curry Glazed Ducks, 111

D

Danish-pickled Spruce Grouse, 55
Dijon Pheasant Legs, 22
Dove Breast & Pear Salad, 74
Dove Breasts in Creamy Pepper Sauce, 71
Dove Pastry Nests, 73
Dove Risotto, 72
Doves in Bread Dressing, 75
Duck & Vegetable Sauté, 123
Duck Breasts with Whiskey-Peppercorn
Sauce, 98
Duck Cassoulet, 110
Duck Diane, 114
Duck Mole, 116
Duck Mulligatawny, 118
Duck Risotto, 105
Ducks with Orange Sauce, 95
Duck Tortilla Torte, 108
Duck Wellington, 123
Duck with Honey-Chili Glaze, 112

E

Easy Pheasant Pie, 26

F

Fast Dishes,
Artichoke & Parmesan Stuffed Partridge
Rolls, 51
Blackened Duck, 114
Cranberry-Jalapeño Glazed Duck Breast, 98
Duck Breasts with Whiskey-Peppercorn
Sauce, 98
Duck Diane, 114
Duck Tortilla Torte, 108
Easy Pheasant Pie, 26
Orange Pecan Rice, 120
Pheasant with Dried Cherries & Pecans, 21
Raspberry-Sherry Glazed Ruffed Grouse, 33
Ruffed Grouse with Chestnuts &
Cranberries, 35
Sage Grouse Soup with Dumplings, 56
Snap Pea Sauté, 120
Tea-smoked Duck, 99
White Pheasant Pizza with Roasted Red
Pepper, 27

Wild Rice Pheasant Soup, 26
Fennel-braised Blue Grouse, 37
Five-spice Duck Stir-fry, 101
Five-spice Prairie Chicken, 54
Focaccia, Herbed, 31
Fresh Duck Sausage, 105
Fried/Sautéed Dishes,
  Apple-Apricot Quail Couscous, 67
  Apple Cider Partridge, 39
  Apple-Ginger Ruffed Grouse, 32
  Blackened Duck, 114
  Cajun Pheasant Fingers, 22
  Chicken-fried Pheasant, 14
  Chukar Partridge with Lentils, 43
  Chutney-Ginger Sharptail, 46
  Duck Breasts with Whiskey-Peppercorn
    Sauce, 98
  Duck Diane, 114
  Fresh Duck Sausage, 105
  Herb & Cheese Stuffed Chukar Breasts, 40
  Herbed Sharptail Sauté, 46
  Hungarian Partridge Scaloppini, 49
  Parmesan Pheasant, 24
  Peach Doves & Rice, 73
  Pheasant Fajitas, 25
  Pheasant Saltimbocca, 23
  Pheasant with Dried Cherries & Pecans, 21
  Pheasant with Sun-dried Tomatoes & Pine
    Nuts, 24
  Pineapple Quail Sauté, 67
  Portobello Quail, 62
  Prairie Chicken & Roasted Peppers, 53
  Ruffed Grouse with Chestnuts &
    Cranberries, 35
  Raspberry-Sherry Glazed Ruffed Grouse, 33
  Sage Grouse with Artichokes &
    Mushrooms, 57
  Sautéed Ruffed Grouse with Thyme, 41
  Sautéed Wood Duck with Balsamic-Date
    Sauce, 107
  Straw & Hay, 107
Fruit,
  Dove Breast & Pear Salad, 74
  Fruit-braised Goose Breast, 83
  Fruity Garlic-roasted Pheasant, 19
  Ruffed Grouse Fruit Salad, 35
  Winter Fruit Dressing, 80
  See also individual fruits
Fruit-braised Goose Breast, 83
Fruity Garlic-roasted Pheasant, 19

G

Garlic Mashed Potatoes, 14
Goose Cacciatore, 87
Goose Jerky, 85
Goose Lasagna Casserole, 93
Goose Pot Pie, 87
Goose Salad Sandwiches, 90
Grape Leaf Wrapped Quail, 63
Gravy, see: Sauces and Gravies
Grilled Dishes,
  Calvados Duck, 111
  Curry Glazed Ducks, 111
  Fresh Duck Sausage, 105
  Grilled Doves, 74
  Grilled Duck with Pepper Jelly Glaze, 115
  Grilled Quail & Sweet Potatoes, 64
  Grill-smoked Chukar Partridge, 41
  Grill-smoked Duck, 97
  Grill-smoked Pheasant, 18

Hunan Duck, 118
Lemon & Rosemary Duck Breasts, 112
Moroccan Grilled Sharptail, 47
Orange Duck Salad with Toasted
  Almonds, 122
Oriental Barbecued Goose Kabobs, 86
Oriental Grilled Quail, 69
Red-wine Marinated Spruce Grouse, 57
Ruffed Grouse Fruit Salad, 35
Sweet & Hot Glazed Chukars, 38
Grilled Doves, 74
Grilled Duck with Pepper Jelly Glaze, 115
Grilled Quail & Sweet Potatoes, 64
Grill-smoked Chukar Partridge, 41
Grill-smoked Duck, 97
Grill-smoked Pheasant, 18
Gumbo, 117

H

Herb & Cheese Stuffed Chukar Breasts, 40
Herb-coated Roast Pheasant, 16
Herbed Focaccia, 31
Herbed Sharptail Sauté, 46
Horseradish-Ginger Duck Breasts, 99
Horseradish Prairie Chicken, 52
Hot & Sour Duck Soup, 102
Hunan Duck, 118
Hungarian Partridge Hunter's Style, 48
Hungarian Partridge Scaloppini, 49
Hungarian Partridge with Juniper, 48

I

Indian Dishes,
  Chutney-Ginger Sharptail, 46
  Cranberry-Apple Chutney, 58
  Curried Goose & Spinach, 89
  Duck Mulligatawny, 118
Italian Dishes,
  Artichoke & Parmesan Stuffed Partridge
    Rolls, 51
  Dove Risotto, 72
  Duck Risotto, 105
  Goose Cacciatore, 87
  Herbed Focaccia, 31
  Hungarian Partridge Scaloppini, 49
  Pheasant Saltimbocca, 23
  Polenta Quail, 61
  Portobello Quail, 62
  Risotto Grouse Casserole, 42
  Straw & Hay, 107

J

Jambalaya, 119
Juniper Berries,
  Calvados Duck, 111
  Danish-pickled Spruce Grouse, 55
  Hungarian Partridge Hunter's Style, 48
  Hungarian Partridge with Juniper, 48

L

Lasagna Casserole, Goose, 93
Lemon & Rosemary Duck Breasts, 112
Lemon-Honey Ruffed Grouse, 33
Lemon-Rosemary Chukar Partridge, 37
Lentils, Chukar Partridge with, 43
Low-fat Dishes,
  Apple-Ginger Ruffed Grouse, 32
  Barbecued Goose Sandwiches, 91

Billy's Spicy Oriental Sharptail, 44
Cranberry-Apple Chutney, 58
Cranberry-Jalapeño Glazed Duck Breast, 98
Creamed Pheasant & Biscuits, 19
Danish-pickled Spruce Grouse, 55
Duck Mulligatawny, 118
Duck with Honey-Chili Glaze, 112
Five-spice Duck Stir-fry, 101
Five-spice Prairie Chicken, 54
Goose Cacciatore, 87
Goose Jerky, 85
Hot & Sour Duck Soup, 102
Hunan Duck, 118
Lemon & Rosemary Duck Breasts, 112
Lemon-Honey Ruffed Grouse, 33
Pheasant Fajitas, 25
Prairie Chicken & Vegetable Soup, 54
Pumpkin Soup, 11
Red-wine Marinated Spruce Grouse, 57
Ruffed Grouse with Chestnuts &
  Cranberries, 35
Sautéed Ruffed Grouse with Thyme, 41
Sautéed Wood Duck with Balsamic-Date
  Sauce, 107
Smoked Goose & Vegetable Soup, 92
Smoky Split Pea & Goose Soup, 92
Turkey Chowder, 13
Wild Rice Pheasant Soup, 26
Woodcock Rumaki, 76

M

Main Dishes,
  Apple-Apricot Quail Couscous, 67
  Apple Cider Partridge, 39
  Apple-Ginger Ruffed Grouse, 32
  Apricot-glazed Goose, 83
  Artichoke & Parmesan Stuffed Partridge
    Rolls, 51
  Barbecue-smoked Turkey, 12
  Billy's Spicy Oriental Sharptail, 44
  Blackberry-Duck Salad, 106
  Blackened Duck, 114
  Blue Grouse Madeira with Chutney, 36
  Broiled Quail, 58
  Calvados Duck, 111
  Cherry-sauced Quail, 63
  Chicken-fried Pheasant, 14
  Chukar Partridge in Rosemary-Cream
    Sauce, 39
  Chukar Partridge with Lentils, 43
  Chukar Partridge with Pears, 31
  Chutney-Ginger Sharptail, 46
  Cranberry-glazed Pheasant, 17
  Cranberry-Jalapeño Glazed Duck Breast, 98
  Cranberry-Pheasant Wild Rice Salad, 28
  Creamed Pheasant & Biscuits, 19
  Creamy Ruffed Grouse with Rosemary, 34
  Creole Duck, 113
  Currant-Mustard Goose Breast, 85
  Curried Goose & Spinach, 89
  Curry Glazed Ducks, 111
  Dove Breast & Pear Salad, 74
  Dove Breasts in Creamy Pepper Sauce, 71
  Dove Pastry Nests, 73
  Dove Risotto, 72
  Doves in Bread Dressing, 75
  Duck & Vegetable Sauté, 123
  Duck Breasts with Whiskey-Peppercorn
    Sauce, 98
  Duck Diane, 114
  Duck Mole, 116
  Duck Risotto, 105
  Ducks with Orange Sauce, 95
  Duck Tortilla Torte, 108
  Duck Wellington, 123
  Duck with Honey-Chili Glaze, 112

Easy Pheasant Pie, 26
Fennel-braised Blue Grouse, 37
Five-spice Duck Stir-fry, 101
Five-spice Prairie Chicken, 54
Fruit-braised Goose Breast, 83
Fruity Garlic-roasted Pheasant, 19
Goose Cacciatore, 87
Grape Leaf Wrapped Quail, 63
Grill-smoked Chukar Partridge, 41
Grill-smoked Duck, 97
Grill-smoked Pheasant, 18
Grilled Doves, 74
Grilled Duck with Pepper Jelly Glaze, 115
Grilled Quail & Sweet Potatoes, 64
Gumbo, 117
Herb & Cheese Stuffed Chukar Breasts, 40
Herb-coated Roast Pheasant, 16
Herbed Sharptail Sauté, 46
Horseradish-Ginger Duck Breasts, 99
Horseradish Prairie Chicken, 52
Hunan Duck, 118
Hungarian Partridge Hunter's Style, 48
Hungarian Partridge Scaloppini, 49
Hungarian Partridge with Juniper, 48
Jambalaya, 119
Lemon & Rosemary Duck Breasts, 112
Lemon-Honey Ruffed Grouse, 33
Lemon-Rosemary Chukar Partridge, 37
Marinated Pheasant Salad, 29
Mediterranean Pheasant with Onions, 20
Minted Blue Grouse, 36
Moroccan Goose Couscous, 91
Moroccan Grilled Sharptail, 47
Orange & Chili Glazed Goose, 82
Orange Duck Salad with Toasted
    Almonds, 122
Orange Ruffed Grouse, 32
Oriental Barbecued Goose Kabobs, 86
Oriental Goose Salad, 89
Oriental Grilled Quail, 69
Parmesan Pheasant, 24
Peach Doves & Rice, 73
Peach-sauced Quail, 68
Pecan Turkey with Maple Sauce, 12
Peppered Partridge Paprikash, 50
Pheasant Fajitas, 25
Pheasant Saltimbocca, 23
Pheasant with Dried Cherries & Pecans, 21
Pheasant with Sun-dried Tomatoes & Pine
    Nuts, 24
Pineapple Quail Sauté, 67
Polenta Quail, 61
Portobello Quail, 62
Prairie Chicken & Roasted Peppers, 53
Quail en Papillote, 65
Quail with Apricot Dressing, 68
Raspberry-glazed Ducks, 120
Raspberry-Sherry Glazed Ruffed Grouse, 33
Red-wine Marinated Spruce Grouse, 57
Roast Goose, 80
Roast Quail with Sherry Crumbs & Cream
    Sauce, 60
Roasted Prairie Chicken with Potatoes, 53
Roasted Wild Turkey, 11
Rosemary-Garlic Quail with Baby Squash, 66
Ruffed Grouse Fruit Salad, 35
Ruffed Grouse with Chestnuts &
    Cranberries, 35
Sage Grouse with Artichokes &
    Mushrooms, 57
Sage Grouse with Figs & Apricots, 55
Sautéed Ruffed Grouse with Thyme, 41
Sautéed Wood Duck with Balsamic-Date
    Sauce, 107
Sherry-Cream Pheasant, 21
Smoke-cooked Herbed Quail, 65
Smoked Duck Hash Packets, 104
Spicy Stir-fried Woodcock, 76
Straw & Hay, 107
Sun-dried Tomato Duck Breasts, 102

Sweet & Hot Glazed Chukars, 38
Sweet & Sour Duck, 100
Tea-smoked Duck, 99
Traditional Roast Duck with Dressing, 96
Turkey Stew with Dumplings, 13
White Pheasant Pizza with Roasted Red
    Pepper, 27
Wood Duck with Apples & Apricots, 106
Marinated Pheasant Salad, 29
Mediterranean Pheasant with Onions, 20
Mexican Dishes,
    Duck Mole, 116
    Duck Tortilla Torte, 108
    Pheasant Fajitas, 25
Middle-Eastern Dishes,
    Apple-Apricot Quail Couscous, 67
    Moroccan Goose Couscous, 91
    Moroccan Grilled Sharptail, 47
Minted Blue Grouse, 36
Moroccan Goose Couscous, 91
Moroccan Grilled Sharptail, 47
Mushrooms,
    Creole Duck, 113
    Dove Breasts in Creamy Pepper Sauce, 71
    Dove Pastry Nests, 73
    Doves in Bread Dressing, 75
    Duck & Vegetable Sauté, 123
    Duck Wellington, 123
    Goose Cacciatore, 87
    Hot & Sour Duck Soup, 102
    Oriental Goose Salad, 89
    Portobello Quail, 62
    Quail en Papillote, 65
    Risotto Grouse Casserole, 42
    Sage Grouse with Artichokes &
        Mushrooms, 57
    Sherry-Cream Pheasant, 21
    Spicy Stir-fried Woodcock, 76
    Teal Eggroll Triangles, 122

O

Orange & Chili Glazed Goose, 82
Orange Duck Salad with Toasted Almonds, 122
Orange Pecan Rice, 120
Orange Ruffed Grouse, 32
Oriental Barbecued Goose Kabobs, 86
Oriental Dishes,
    Billy's Spicy Oriental Sharptail, 44
    Five-spice Duck Stir-fry, 101
    Five-spice Prairie Chicken, 54
    Hot & Sour Duck Soup, 102
    Hunan Duck, 118
    Oriental Barbecued Goose Kabobs, 86
    Oriental Duck Soup, 103
    Oriental Goose Salad, 89
    Oriental Grilled Quail, 69
    Spicy Stir-fried Woodcock, 76
    Sweet & Sour Duck, 100
    Teal Eggroll Triangles, 122
    Tea-smoked Duck, 99
    Woodcock Rumaki, 76
Oriental Duck Soup, 103
Oriental Goose Salad, 89
Oriental Grilled Quail, 69

P

Parmesan Pheasant, 24
Pasta,
    Dove Breasts in Creamy Pepper Sauce, 71
    Duck & Vegetable Sauté, 123

Goose Lasagna Casserole, 93
Peppered Partridge Paprikash, 50
Pheasant with Sun-dried Tomatoes & Pine
    Nuts, 24
Straw & Hay, 107
Pastry,
    Dove Pastry Nests, 73
    Duck Wellington, 123
    Easy Pheasant Pie, 26
    Pie Crust, 87
    Smoked Duck Hash Packets, 104
    See also: Pot Pies
Pâté, Woodcock, 77
Peach Doves & Rice, 73
Peach-sauced Quail, 68
Pecans,
    Orange Pecan Rice, 120
    Pecan Turkey with Maple Sauce, 12
    Pheasant with Dried Cherries & Pecans, 21
Pecan Turkey with Maple Sauce, 12
Peppered Partridge Paprikash, 50
Pepper Jelly Glaze, Grilled Duck with, 115
Peppers,
    Creole Duck, 113
    Dove Breasts in Creamy Pepper Sauce, 71
    Gumbo, 117
    Oriental Barbecued Goose Kabobs, 86
    Oriental Grilled Quail, 69
    Peppered Partridge Paprikash, 50
    Pineapple Quail Sauté, 67
    Roasting red peppers, 27
    White Pheasant Pizza with Roasted Red
        Pepper, 27
    See also: Chilies/Chili Peppers
Pheasant Fajitas, 25
Pheasant Saltimbocca, 23
Pheasant with Dried Cherries & Pecans, 21
Pheasant with Sun-dried Tomatoes & Pine
    Nuts, 24
Pie Crust, 87
Pineapple Quail Sauté, 67
Pizza, White Pheasant, with Roasted Red
    Pepper, 27
Polenta Quail, 61
Portobello Quail, 62
Potato Galette with Chive Sour Cream, 95
Pot Pies,
    Easy Pheasant Pie, 26
    Goose Pot Pie, 87
Prairie Chicken & Roasted Peppers, 53
Prairie Chicken & Vegetable Soup, 54
Pumpkin Soup, 11

Q

Quail en Papillote, 65
Quail with Apricot Dressing, 68

R

Raspberry-glazed Ducks, 120
Raspberry-Sherry Glazed Ruffed Grouse, 33
Red-wine Marinated Spruce Grouse, 57
Rice,
    Blue Grouse Madeira with Chutney, 36
    Creole Duck, 113
    Curried Goose & Spinach, 89
    Dove Risotto, 72
    Duck Mole, 116
    Duck Risotto, 105
    Five-spice Duck Stir-fry, 101
    Goose Cacciatore, 87

Gumbo, 117
Jambalaya, 119
Orange Pecan Rice, 120
Oriental Barbecued Goose Kabobs, 86
Peach Doves & Rice, 73
Risotto Grouse Casserole, 42
Sherry-Cream Pheasant, 21
Spanish Rice & Goose Casserole, 93
Spicy Stir-fried Woodcock, 76
Zesty Goose & Rice Casserole, 88
See also: Wild Rice
Rice Powder, Preparing, 101
Risotto Grouse Casserole, 42
Roasted Dishes,
  Apricot-glazed Goose, 83
  Chukar Partridge with Pears, 31
  Cranberry-glazed Pheasant, 17
  Currant-Mustard Goose Breast, 85
  Ducks with Orange Sauce, 95
  Fruit-braised Goose Breast, 83
  Fruity Garlic-roasted Pheasant, 19
  Herb-coated Roast Pheasant, 16
  Horseradish Prairie Chicken, 52
  Lemon-Honey Ruffed Grouse, 33
  Orange & Chili Glazed Goose, 82
  Orange Ruffed Grouse, 32
  Polenta Quail, 61
  Raspberry-glazed Ducks, 120
  Roasted Prairie Chicken with Potatoes, 53
  Roasted Wild Turkey, 11
  Roast Goose, 80
  Roast Quail with Sherry Crumbs & Cream Sauce, 60
  Traditional Roast Duck with Dressing, 96
  Wood Duck with Apples & Apricots, 106
Roasted Prairie Chicken with Potatoes, 53
Roasted Wild Turkey, 11
Roast Goose, 80
Roast Quail with Sherry Crumbs & Cream Sauce, 60
Rosemary-Garlic Quail with Baby Squash, 66
Ruffed Grouse Fruit Salad, 35
Ruffed Grouse with Chestnuts & Cranberries, 35
Rumaki, Woodcock, 76

S

Sage Grouse Soup with Dumplings, 56
Sage Grouse with Artichokes & Mushrooms, 57
Sage Grouse with Figs & Apricots, 55
Salads,
  Blackberry-Duck Salad, 106
  Cranberry-Pheasant Wild Rice Salad, 28
  Cucumber-Yogurt Salad, 44
  Dove Breast & Pear Salad, 74
  Goose Salad Sandwiches, 90
  Marinated Pheasant Salad, 29
  Orange Duck Salad with Toasted Almonds, 122
  Oriental Goose Salad, 89
  Oriental Grilled Quail, 69
  Ruffed Grouse Fruit Salad, 35
  Tricolored Salad, 108
Sauces and Gravies,
  Cherry-sauced Quail, 63
  Chicken-fried Pheasant Gravy, 14
  Doves in Bread Dressing, 75

Duck Breasts with Whiskey-Peppercorn Sauce, 98
Duck Diane, 114
Duck Mole, 116
Polenta Quail, 61
Sautéed Wood Duck with Balsamic-Date Sauce, 107
Smoked Duck Hash Packets, 104
Sweet & Sour Duck, 100
Sausage,
  Duck Cassoulet, 110
  Fresh Duck Sausage, 105
  Gumbo, 117
  Hungarian Partridge Hunter's Style, 48
  Jambalaya, 119
  Smoked Duck Hash Packets, 104
Sautéed Dishes, see: Fried/Sautéed Dishes
Sautéed Ruffed Grouse with Thyme, 41
Sautéed Wood Duck with Balsamic-Date Sauce, 107
Sharptail Soup with Caraway Dumplings, 47
Sherry-Cream Pheasant, 21
Side Dishes, see: Accompaniments and Side Dishes
Smoke-cooked Herbed Quail, 65
Smoked Dishes/Dishes with Smoked Game Birds,
  Barbecue-smoked Turkey, 12
  Goose Jerky, 85
  Grill-smoked Chukar Partridge, 41
  Grill-smoked Duck, 97
  Grill-smoked Pheasant, 18
  How to monitor smoking temperature, 18
  Smoke-cooked Herbed Quail, 65
  Smoked Duck Hash Packets, 104
  Smoked Goose, 84
  Smoked Goose & Vegetable Soup, 92
  Smoky Split Pea & Goose Soup, 92
  Tea-smoked Duck, 99
Smoked Duck Hash Packets, 104
Smoked Goose, 84
Smoked Goose & Vegetable Soup, 92
Smoky Split Pea & Goose Soup, 92
Snap Pea Sauté, 120
Soups and Chowders,
  Creamy Wild Rice-Duck Soup, 103
  Duck Mulligatawny, 118
  Hot & Sour Duck Soup, 102
  Oriental Duck Soup, 103
  Prairie Chicken & Vegetable Soup, 54
  Pumpkin Soup, 11
  Sage Grouse Soup with Dumplings, 56
  Sharptail Soup with Caraway Dumplings, 47
  Smoked Goose & Vegetable Soup, 92
  Smoky Split Pea & Goose Soup, 92
  Turkey Chowder, 13
  Wild Rice Pheasant Soup, 26
  See also: Stews
Spanish Rice & Goose Casserole, 93
Spicy Stir-fried Woodcock, 76
Squash,
  Chutney-Ginger Sharptail, 46
  Duck & Vegetable Sauté, 123
  Duck Cassoulet, 110
  Rosemary-Garlic Quail with Baby Squash, 66
Stews,
  Jambalaya, 119
  Sage Grouse Soup with Dumplings, 56
  Sharptail Soup with Caraway Dumplings, 47

Turkey Stew with Dumplings, 13
  See also: Soups and Chowders
Stir-fried Dishes,
  Billy's Spicy Oriental Sharptail, 44
  Curried Goose & Spinach, 89
  Five-spice Duck Stir-fry, 101
  Spicy Stir-fried Woodcock, 76
  Sweet & Sour Duck, 100
  Straw & Hay, 107
  Sun-dried Tomato Duck Breasts, 102
Sun-dried Tomatoes,
  Pheasant with Sun-dried Tomatoes & Pine Nuts, 24
  Rehydrating dried tomatoes, 24
  Sun-dried Tomato Duck Breasts, 102
Sweet & Hot Glazed Chukars, 38
Sweet & Sour Duck, 100
Sweet Potatoes, Grilled Quail &, 64

T

Teal Eggroll Triangles, 122
Tea-smoked Duck, 99
Traditional Roast Duck with Dressing, 96
Tricolored Salad, 108
Trussing a Pheasant, 16
Turkey Chowder, 13
Turkey Stew with Dumplings, 13

V

Very Fast Dishes,
  Barbecued Goose Sandwiches, 91
  Cajun Pheasant Fingers, 22
  Creamy Wild Rice Duck Soup, 103
  Curried Goose & Spinach, 89
  Curry Glazed Ducks, 111
  Dove Breast & Pear Salad, 74
  Duck & Vegetable Sauté, 123
  Five-spice Stir-fry, 101
  Herbed Sharptail Sauté, 46
  Hot & Sour Duck Soup, 46
  Hungarian Partridge Hunter's Style, 48
  Moroccan Goose Couscous, 91
  Orange Duck Salad with Toasted Almonds, 122
  Oriental Duck Soup, 103
  Oriental Goose Salad, 89
  Parmesan Pheasant, 24
  Pheasant Saltimbocca, 23
  Prairie Chicken & Roasted Peppers, 53
  Raspberry-glazed Ducks, 120
  Ruffed Grouse Fruit Salad, 35
  Spicy Stir-fried Woodcock, 76
  Straw & Hay, 107
  Sun-dried Tomato Duck Breasts, 102

W

White Pheasant Pizza with Roasted Red Pepper, 27
Wild Rice,
  Cranberry-Pheasant Wild Rice Salad, 28
  Creamy Wild Rice-Duck Soup, 103
  Wild Rice Pheasant Soup, 26
Wild Rice Pheasant Soup, 26
Winter Fruit Dressing, 80
Woodcock Pâté, 77
Woodcock Rumaki, 76
Wood Duck with Apples & Apricots, 106

Creative Publishing international is the most complete source of How-To Information for the Outdoorsman

THE COMPLETE HUNTER™ *Series*

- *Advanced Whitetail Hunting*
- *America's Favorite Wild Game Recipes*
- *Bowhunting Equipment & Skills*
- *The Complete Guide to Hunting*
- *Cooking Wild in Kate's Kitchen*
- *Dressing & Cooking Wild Game*
- *Duck Hunting*
- *Elk Hunting*
- *Game Bird Cookery*
- *Mule Deer Hunting*
- *Muzzleloading*
- *Pronghorn Hunting*
- *Upland Game Birds*
- *Venison Cookery*
- *Whitetail Deer*
- *Wild Turkey*

The Freshwater Angler™ *Series*

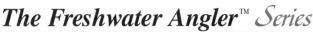

- *Advanced Bass Fishing*
- *All-Time Favorite Fish Recipes*
- *The Art of Fly Tying*
- *The Art of Freshwater Fishing*
- *Fishing for Catfish*
- *Fishing Rivers & Streams*
- *Fishing Tips & Tricks*
- *Fishing With Artificial Lures*
- *Fishing With Live Bait*
- *Fly Fishing for Trout in Streams*
- *Largemouth Bass*
- *Modern Methods of Ice Fishing*
- *The New Cleaning & Cooking Fish*
- *Northern Pike & Muskie*
- *Panfish*
- *Smallmouth Bass*
- *Successful Walleye Fishing*
- *Trout*

The Complete FLY FISHERMAN™ *Series*

- *Fishing Dry Flies – Surface Presentations for Trout in Streams*
- *Fishing Nymphs, Wet Flies & Streamers – Subsurface Techniques for Trout in Streams*
- *Fly-Fishing Equipment & Skills*
- *Fly-Tying Techniques & Patterns*

To purchase these or other titles, contact your local bookseller, call **1-800-328-3895** or visit our web site at **www.howtobookstore.com**

For a list of participating retailers near you, call 1-800-328-0590